THE PHONE BOOK

Library of Congress Control Number: 2022951825

ISBN: 9781641709903
eISBN: 9781641709224
KF: 9781641709231
FE: 9781641709217

Printed in the United States of America

Edited by Abigail W. Tree, Sarah Echard, and Mikaela Sircable
Cover design by Mara Harris
Book design by Mara Harris

10 9 8 7 6 5 4 3 2 1

THE PHONE BOOK

Stay Safe, Be Smart, and Make the World Better with the Powerful Device in Your Hand

by Jessica Speer

Illustrations by Lesley Imgart

To Mom. Thank you for your unwavering support and for always seeing the best in me. And to the everyday heroes who design and use technology in ways that make the world a better, kinder place.

CONTENTS

Introduction 1

Chapter 1:

Why Tech Companies Want You Staring at Your Screen ...7

Chapter 2:

Your Digital Footprint (aka Your Digital Reputation)........23

Chapter 3:

Detecting Disinformation—

Sleuthing Truth from Lies and Fake Stuff 37

Chapter 4:

Social Media—Welcome to Disneyland................................49

Chapter 5:

FOMO, FOJI, and Text Slang Galore 65

Chapter 6:

Zombie Land—Is Tech Addiction a Thing? 77

Chapter 7:

Creepy People—Stranger Danger Online 91

Chapter 8:

Cyberbullying and Digital Drama, Ugh 103

Chapter 9:

Bonus Activities! Techy Tidbits, Weird Facts,

Trivia & Definitions Revisited..119

Chapter 10:

You and Your Phone—A Force for Good 127

A Note to Caregivers 135

References 137

About the Author 157

About Familius 158

INTRODUCTION

Think back to the day you got your phone. It was love at first sight. Rainbows, chirping birds, and harp music filled the air. Okay, maybe not. But you were psyched. Little did you know that your shiny, new device is powerful. A lightsaber to be used for good or for the dark side.

Seriously, smartphones are REALLY powerful! Did you know that your smartphone has more computing power than the computers used for the Apollo 11 moon landing? But did you also know that the more hours teens spend on their phones, the more likely they are to experience depression?

Geez, imagine all that power right in your pocket—power to be used as a force for good or, um, not so good. Okay, or for downright sad, awkward, or nasty stuff. You have to admit, it's sort of funny that these devices come without a warning label. But considering the history of cigarettes, cars without seat belts, and other inventions that hit the market without warning labels, it's not that surprising.

Hence the need for this book. Through real stories, weird facts, and techy tidbits, this book reveals the power of your phone as well as your superpower to slay the dark side of technology. You will learn how to detect disinformation and fake stuff, how to stomp out cyberbullying, how to protect your privacy and digital reputation, and much more.

Go forth, read, and be informed. May the force be with you.

CAUTION: If you regularly experience **myötähäpeä**, some of the stories in this book might make you feel a wee bit uncomfortable. Have no fear. Discomfort is an opportunity for growth. Or, it's just uncomfortable.

DEFINITION:

Myötähäpeä (noun): the feeling of embarrassment you experience on behalf of another person when they do something foolish.

CHAPTER ROADMAP

Um, what are you waiting for? Reading a book about your phone is not how you planned to spend your day? Yeah, yeah. I totally get it. You would rather crack secret codes, read "real" stories, or hang out with kids your age.

Well, this is your lucky day! Grab a pencil, polish up your sleuthing skills, and get ready to dive in because each chapter includes all those things and more. Here is a road map of what you'll find in this book.

SCREEN STORIES

These stories feature things that actually happened to people when they were using technology. Some stories are positive and inspiring. Others—well—let's just say they share valuable lessons learned. All these stories offer insight into today's tech-centered world.

TEST YOUR KNOWLEDGE

Each chapter includes some true or false or fill-in-the-blank questions to test your knowledge about phones and technology. But don't worry! These tests are not for a grade. They simply get you thinking about each topic.

REALITY CHECK

Grab some colored pencils or markers. These sections include hands-on activities to practice what you have learned and games to have some fun.

STRAIGHT TALK FROM TEENS

The best advice often comes from those with experience. Straight Talk from Teens shares nuggets of wisdom from your phone-owning peers. Feel free to add your ideas to this collection of sage advice.

CRACK THE SECRET CODE

In each chapter, you'll have a chance to crack a secret code that reveals ways to hone your superpowers. From Morse code to emoji code, see if you can unlock them all!

HEALTHY & SAFE HABITS CHECKLIST

Owning a phone comes with a lot of choices and responsibilities. These handy checklists include ways to keep your phone use healthy and safe.

But wait, there's more! Scattered throughout the book are facts, tidbits, and definitions that will help you understand and master the mysteries of technology. There is power in knowledge. And this knowledge, young Jedi, will help you control the force within your phone and use it for good.

📱 TECHY TIDBITS

These tidbits explain tech terms and trends in our ever-changing digital world.

👽 WEIRD FACTS

These facts feature perplexing, entertaining, and weird stuff that happens on or with phones.

📌 DEFINITIONS

And last but not least, this book would not be complete without loads of definitions.

Let's do this!

Disclaimer: To protect privacy, names and details in some stories have been changed.

CHAPTER 1:

WHY TECH COMPANIES WANT YOU STARING AT YOUR SCREEN

"Life doesn't give us purpose. We give life purpose."
—The Flash

"Phones don't give us purpose. We give phones purpose."
—Yours Truly :)

SCREEN STORY: GAVIN'S LOST MORNING

Gavin's two favorite things are soccer and technology. When he's not scoring goals on the field, he loves watching videos, playing games, and connecting with friends online.

On Saturday, Gavin's phone buzzes him awake. His friends want him to join their video game. He dives right in and plays for an hour before his mom calls him downstairs for breakfast. As he logs out, he notices a bunch of DMs on social media. He responds and then scrolls through his feed. One post links to a video of dogs doing tricks. He watches a few more.

Another half hour passes. His mom calls him to eat again. While closing the videos to head downstairs, Gavin sees a Snapchat notification reminding him about his 92-day streak. So he quickly takes a Snap. His mom, now fuming, storms into his room and takes his phone. He's going to be late for his soccer game.

Gavin throws on his uniform, grabs his soccer bag, and glances at the clock. His game starts in 15 minutes. So much for breakfast. He grabs a banana on his way out the door. Hopefully he has everything he needs.

Where did Gavin's morning go?

That's a simple question with a not-so-simple answer. The obvious answer is that Gavin spent his morning on his phone. Duh. The complicated answer is that he spent his morning putting cash in the pockets of tech companies with his screen time. Cha-ching! Here's how.

Most search engines, games, videos, and social media apps are "free," but they are not really free. Many tech companies collect user data and sell ad space to other companies to make money. YouTube, social media, and games profit from advertising.

As Gavin scrolled through his feed, watched videos, and played games, he saw ads placed by companies who were hoping to sell him stuff. Companies spend BILLIONS of dollars each year to reach kids and teens like Gavin with ads. Ads for new shoes, new games, new snacks. Ads for just about everything! The more time you spend on your screen, the more ad space tech companies sell and the more money they make. Who knew your eyeballs were worth so much?

> **Your screen time + ads sold to companies = $$$ for tech companies!**

Since screen time equals money, it makes sense that tech companies want to keep eyes on devices. So how do they keep people looking at screens? Like any magician, companies have tricks up their sleeves. Abracadabra! Introducing . . . **persuasive design**.

📌 **DEFINITION:**

Persuasive design (noun): technology designed to change users' attitudes or behaviors.
(Hmmm, that sounds sort of creepy!)

 **TECHY TIDBIT:**

Here are some persuasive design techniques used to increase screen time.

- **Tags**—Tagging others in posts alerts the tagged people, who then check the post.
- **Notifications**—These alerts and reminders draw users back to apps.
- **Streaks**—Streaks require users to post daily to keep the streak going.
- **Rewards**—Rewards, such as tokens, coins, and new levels, keep users playing.
- **In-app ads**—Users must watch ads to continue playing or watching.

Geez, that helps to explain why it's so hard to put your phone down!

TEST YOUR KNOWLEDGE—SCREEN TIME

Let's see how much you know about your screen time. Please answer these true or false questions. Don't worry. This is not for a grade!

1. **True or False:** What you do on your phone, such as what you search for, what games you play, and what videos you watch, stays private.

2. **True or False:** Most video games and apps are designed with your health and wellness in mind.

3. **True or False:** You can change your phone settings and habits to reduce the effect of persuasive design tricks.

Quiz Answers:

1. False. Search engines, apps, social media, and games collect data about online habits. This data is often used for advertising.

2. False. Because more screen time = more profit, many tech companies prioritize keeping people on screens longer. This is not the best news for your health.

3. True (phew!). Keep reading and see the end-of-chapter checklist for tips.

REALITY CHECK—SCREEN TIME

Many games, videos, and apps are awesome! However, it's easy to forget all of the other awesome things in life while you are staring at your screen. As you manage your tech use, it helps to understand the difference between mindful and mindless screen time.

Mindful Screen Time	Mindless Screen Time
1. Sending messages to connect with people	1. Making fun of other people's posts
2. Watching videos to learn new things and find information	2. Scrolling out of boredom
3. Playing games with friends or family	3. Watching things you don't care about
4. Creating art and content	4. Avoiding activities you want or need to do because screen time is easier

When you find yourself lost in mindless screen time, it's a good idea to do something else. On the lines below, write three things you <u>like to do</u> or <u>want to learn</u>. For example, you may like to play guitar, skateboard, draw animals, play basketball, read books, bake cookies, or clean your room. (Okay, maybe not that last one.)

Three Things I Like to Do or Want to Learn:

1.

2.

3.

A USUAL DAY IN YOUR LIFE

Now, let's apply **mindless and mindful screen time** to real life. The circle below represents one day in your life, divided into 24 hours. Think about what your day USUALLY looks like. What do you do? How much time do you spend attending school, sleeping, looking at your screen, or doing other stuff? Use colored pencils or markers to shade and label the circle's hour slices with how you usually spend your time.

(Each slice = one hour of a 24-hour day)

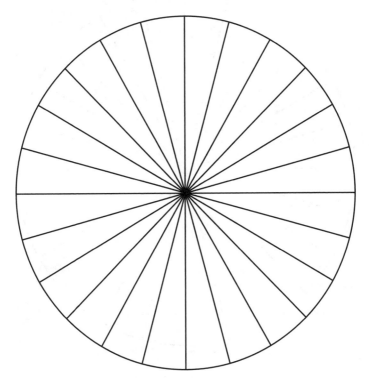

AN IDEAL DAY IN YOUR LIFE

Now think about your IDEAL day. Fill in each hour
slice with how you would like to spend your free time,
including any screen time and other activities you want
to do or learn (Include time for the things you wrote on
page 12.). Be sure to shade the hours you sleep, do chores,
and go to school. But your free time is yours to manage
as you wish.

(Each slice = one hour of a 24-hour day)

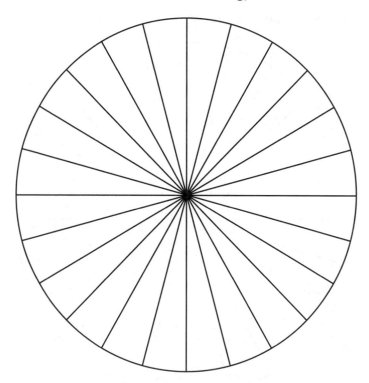

Compare your two circles. How does your USUAL DAY compare to your IDEAL DAY? Would you change anything to make your usual day more like an ideal day? Please write your response below.

_____

_____

_____

 **TECHY TIDBIT:**

Algorithms are ways that search engines, social media, and apps use your old screen behaviors to send you new content, videos, and ads. What you watch, what you "like," and what you do on your phone triggers similar content to keep you on your phone. For example, watching a funny cat video leads to more cat videos. Yay!

👽 **WEIRD FACT:**

Algorithms are designed to show you more of what you like, but this gets weird. Let's say two people each type the same exact question into the same search engine and compare responses. The responses will be different because the results are based on what each person has searched in the past. Hmmm . . . kinda strange that the answers are not the same.

STRAIGHT TALK FROM TEENS:
WHAT DO YOU DO TO KEEP SCREEN TIME
FROM TAKING OVER YOUR LIFE?

With persuasive design, cool games, and apps, it's easy to get lost in screen time. No wonder **phubbing** is at an all-time high! Here's how some teens keep their screen time in check so they can spend time doing other things they want or need to do. Feel free to add your insights too!

I set time limits on apps, social media, and games so I can get my homework and other activities done.

My parents make all of us put our devices away at least an hour before we go to bed each night. If they didn't, I think I would sleep a lot less.

I really want to be a good athlete, which means I need to practice, take care of myself, and sleep. I prioritize that over screen time. Once I finish my training and homework, I relax on my phone.

Your idea:

_____

_____

_____

DEFINITION:

Phubbing (noun): the practice of ignoring the people you are with to pay attention to your phone.

WEIRD FACT:

In Taiwan, parents can be fined $1,600 if their kids spend too much time on screens. Taiwanese lawmakers approved the Child and Youth Welfare and Protection Act, a law modeled after similar laws in China and South Korea that aim to limit screen time to healthy levels.

As you read this chapter, you may wonder why tech companies are allowed to design social media, games, and apps in ways that keep people glued to screens. Why aren't there more laws to protect kids from tech companies? Who is policing the companies' behavior? Efforts are underway to safeguard kids, but lawmaking is a looooong, slowwwww process.

SCREEN STORY: IS THE TIDE TURNING? HOW LAWMAKERS ARE CATCHING UP WITH TECHNOLOGY

In 1998, the US Congress passed the Children's Online Privacy and Protection Act. This law provides some privacy protections for kids under 13, but the law has fallen waaaaayyyy behind the times. Apple's smartphone wasn't even invented until 2007!

However, several US states are starting to update their laws. In 2020, California enacted the Consumer Privacy Rights Act. This law aims to protect privacy, allowing teens more data and privacy options. The law also requires that parents approve any data that tech companies collect on kids younger than 13. In 2022, the European Commission passed a law called the Digital Services Act that requires tech companies to share information about how their algorithms work. This law also prohibits tech companies from targeting kids with advertising.

So stay tuned. Maybe by the time this book hits shelves, more of these laws will be in place!

CRACK THE SECRET CODE—SCREEN TIME

Use the code cracker below to unlock the letters and symbols to spell out the secret phone code. The first word has been completed for you. If you get stuck, see the answer key in Chapter 10.

CODE CRACKER

LETTER/ SYMBOL	CODE	LETTER/ SYMBOL	CODE
A	1	M	14
B	2	N	15
C	3	O	16
D	4	P	17
E	5	Q	18
F	6	R	19
G	7	S	20
H	8	T	21
I	9	U	22
J	10	V	23
K	11	W	24
L	12	Y	25
=	13	$	26

20, 3, 19, 5, 5, 15	SCREEN
21, 9, 14, 5	TIME
13	
26	
6, 16, 19	
21, 5, 3, 8	
2, 22, 21	
25, 16, 22, 19	
21, 9, 14, 5	
9, 20	
25, 16, 22, 19, 20	

After reading this chapter, it may seem like it's you versus voodoo magic tricks when it comes to controlling your screen time. Gulp. But even though persuasive design is tricky, your brain is powerful. You can do a lot to ensure you don't get lost on screens. For example, you might set a timer, or you might not get on your phone until you finish your homework.

What will you do to manage your screen time?

_____

_____

_____

_____

SUMMARY—SCREEN TIME

Because technology moves A LOT faster than lawmakers, many safeguards are not yet in place to protect kids online. This is not surprising. For example, cars didn't have seat belts at first. It took almost a century (and tons of crashes!) before seat belts were invented and required. Now, cars have airbags, safety sensors, and backup cameras. Until more digital safeguards are in place, here are a few tips to keep your screen time in check and to protect your privacy.

SCREEN TIME—HEALTHY & SAFE HABITS CHECKLIST

	Avoid Mindless Screen Time—During screen time, ask yourself, *Am I enjoying this? Is this what I want to be doing right now?*
	Turn Off Notifications—Turn off notifications on apps that distract you from doing other things you could or should be doing.
	Check Privacy Settings—Check your phone settings for options such as "Do not share my data." As laws and rules change, more privacy options may become available.
	X out of Ads—When possible, close ads that pop up on your screen and avoid engaging with ads.

	Delete Old Apps—Delete apps you no longer use so your phone will stop updating them and collecting data.
	Set Limits—Set daily screen limits so you have time to do other activities you enjoy. Avoid keeping your phone in your bedroom while sleeping.

WEIRD PHONE TRIVIA #1

In 1969, astronaut Neil Armstrong stepped out of Apollo 11 and uttered the famous words, "One small step for man, one giant leap for mankind."

Powering Apollo 11 was the Apollo Guidance Computer. It had 32,768 bits of RAM (random access memory). That's not much. Today's phones typically have at least 4GB of RAM. That is 34,359,738,368 bits. This means cell phones have _____ times more RAM memory than the Apollo 11 computer.

A. 10,000 times

B. 100,000 times

C. 1,000,000 times

D. 1,000,000,000 times

Answer: C. 1,000,000! Yes, today's phones have 1 million times more computing power. That makes the Apollo 11 landing in 1969 even more amazing!

CHAPTER 2

YOUR DIGITAL FOOTPRINT (AKA YOUR DIGITAL REPUTATION)

"Heroes are made by the path they choose, not the powers they are graced with." —Iron Man

"Footprints are made on the path you choose and the phone you are graced with." —Yours Truly :)

SCREEN STORY: "I PROMISE I WON'T SHARE IT!"

In 8th grade, Jackson asked Mia out. She was thrilled! They started texting. Soon, Jackson asked her to send some selfies.

One night, he asked Mia to send a private photo of her body. He said that if she truly liked him, she would send one. He promised not to share it with anyone. Mia felt nervous but snapped a photo and sent it anyway.

Two weeks later, Jackson broke up with Mia. After a couple of days, she heard that a semi-nude photo of her was spreading around school. Horrified, she told her mom, who immediately called the principal.

The principal called a meeting with Mia, Jackson, and their parents. Even the police came. The police officers informed them that it's illegal to take and share **nude** photos of kids and teens in Mia's state. They gave Mia and Jackson a stern warning and encouraged them not to make the same mistake again. They deleted the photo from Jackson's phone, but it was already shared. There was no way to get it back.

Mia thought the photo she sent to Jackson would stay private. But nothing shared online is guaranteed to remain private. Nothing. What you do, say, and share online shapes your **digital footprint** or your digital reputation.

Unlike footprints at the beach, your digital footprint doesn't wash away. What you put online is there for the world to find and see. Think of your posts, shares, and comments as a digital scrapbook (or a flashing neon billboard) of your life. Colleges, future employers, teachers, coaches, grandmas, and anyone else with access to the internet can learn about you with just a few keystrokes.

📌 **DEFINITION:**

Digital footprint (noun): information about a particular person that exists on the internet as a result of their online activity.

📌 **DEFINITION:**

Nudes (noun, AKA sexting): a slang term for taking naked or explicit photos and sharing them primarily between mobile phones. Laws vary by state, but taking, sending, and saving nude pictures or videos of people under 18 is a crime in many US states.

TEST YOUR KNOWLEDGE—DIGITAL FOOTPRINTS

Let's see how much you know about digital footprints. Please answer these true or false questions.

1. **True or False:** If you post something to a private account, like your personal Snapchat, it remains within that group.

2. **True or False:** When you delete something online, it no longer exists.

3. **True or False:** Many colleges and employers look up students online to learn about them.

Quiz Answers:

1. False. People can screenshot, save, and share posts anytime.

2. False. A deleted photo or file may still exist. A saved version may remain on the site it was posted, in **the cloud,** or on other devices.

3. True. It's common for colleges and employers to search people online before accepting applications or hiring.

DEFINITION:

The cloud (noun): computer servers that provide data storage and processing on the internet. When something is in "the cloud," it means it's stored on servers around the world instead of your computer or phone's hard drive. (Or, a cloud is simply a mass of water vapor floating in the air :)

REALITY CHECK—DIGITAL FOOTPRINTS

Like it or not, people judge others based on what they see and learn about them online. Photos, memes, likes, comments, and more shape your digital reputation. To explore how this judgement process works, let's play **You Be the Judge**. Then, you can design your digital footprint based on how you plan to shape your digital reputation.

YOU BE THE JUDGE

You are in charge of hiring either Person A or Person B to work in your ice cream shop. After reading each person's stellar application, you check them out online. Here's what you see:

Person A

Person B

Decision time!

Who would you hire? Person A or B? Why?

_____

_____

_____

You may have noticed that you had to make some snap judgments based on images and posts when deciding whom to hire. So yeah, people are told not to "judge a book by its cover," but it happens. Luckily, you can control what you post and share about yourself online. You are the master of your digital reputation, young Jedi.

DESIGN YOUR DIGITAL FOOTPRINT

Grab your colored pencils or markers. Here's your chance to design your very own digital footprint. Add pictures, words, and emojis to the footprint below to showcase how you would like the world to see you. What kind of pictures and videos will you post? What sort of memes will you share? What types of comments will you make? How will you shape your reputation?

Your Digital Footprint

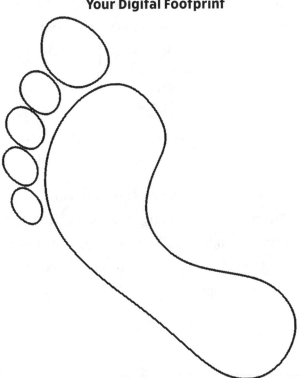

Caution: People often figure out who is behind fake accounts. Social media companies also link people to fake accounts through **IP addresses.**

DEFINITION:

IP Address (noun): Internet Protocol Address. A unique string of numbers identifying a device on the internet or a local network. For example, the wireless internet in your home has a unique IP address, such as 192.158.1.38.

STRAIGHT TALK FROM TEENS:
HOW DO YOU MANAGE YOUR DIGITAL REPUTATION?

Since your digital footprint is on public display, it's essential to consider what you put on the internet. Teens shared what they think about before they post content and how they manage their digital footprint. Feel free to add your insights too!

Some of my friends' parents check their phones. Before I post anything, I remind myself that not just my friends will be seeing it.

I know colleges look at this sort of stuff, so I make sure to post things that show how I want to be seen.

It's hard to control what my friends post about me. Sometimes I ask them not to post some pictures or tag me.

Your thoughts:

_____

_____

_____

SCREEN STORY: BASEBALL BLOGGER TO SPORTS WRITER

In 6th grade, Devan started a baseball blog as a tribute to his grandfather. He and his grandfather loved baseball. Writing helped Devan remember his grandfather and celebrate the sport they loved. In his blog, Devan shared his opinions about players, reviewed games, and reported the latest baseball news. He loved connecting with others who shared his passion.

Over the next few years, Devan gained more skills, like how to maintain a website and gain followers. He became a better writer and shared posts on social media that engaged and inspired others. When Devan graduated from college, he became a professional sports writer. He continues to write about the sport he loves and works to connect with others about baseball. When he started his blog at age 11, he never imagined it would have such an impact on his life.

Not only did Devan's blog help him create a positive digital footprint, but it also helped him gain skills and experience for a career in sports journalism. Now that's a home run! (Corny pun, but I couldn't resist :) How can you, like Devan, use your hobbies and interests to form your digital footprint?

CRACK THE SECRET CODE—DIGITAL REPUTATION

Unscramble the letters in each word to unlock the code. One word has been unscrambled for you to get you started. Yes, it is the shortest word—we didn't want to make this too easy for you! If you get stuck, see the answer key in Chapter 10.

IGHTNON	....
OUY	....
EASHR	....
OENNLI	....
SI	...................IS..................
AVIPRET.	....

SUMMARY—DIGITAL REPUTATION

Your digital reputation matters. What you post, share, and like shapes how people see you and get to know you.

Essentially, what you share online shapes the story of you. Here's a checklist to help you put your best digital footprint forward. (Yeah, another corny pun :)

DIGITAL REPUTATION—HEALTHY & SAFE HABITS CHECKLIST

	Think Before You Post—Remember that your posts are out there for anyone to see, save, and share!
	Be Kind—Avoid harsh, harmful posts that degrade others.
	Keep Your Accounts Private—Keep your social media accounts private. Others may still screenshot what you post, but private accounts limit the number of people viewing your posts.
	Delete Old Accounts—If you no longer use a site or an app, delete your account and then delete the app.
	Choose Strong Passwords—Make sure to use strong passwords and keep them private to avoid anyone else accessing your accounts. People get hacked all the time.
	Ask for Help—If something concerning is posted about you or you post something you wish you hadn't, delete the post, ask for it to be taken down, or get help from a trusted adult.

WEIRD PHONE TRIVIA #2

Millions of phones are damaged every year. According to statistica.com, 26% of phones are damaged because . . .

    A. they were dropped on the ground

    B. they were frozen

    C. they fell in the toilet

    D. they were run over by cars

Answer: C. They fell in the toilet. Most phones are damaged by being dropped on the ground, but 26% are damaged because they fall in the toilet. Ew!

CHAPTER 3:

DETECTING DISINFORMATION— SLEUTHING TRUTH FROM LIES AND FAKE STUFF

"It's easier to fool people than to convince them they have been fooled."—Mark Twain

. (Actually, after fact-checking, there is no proof that Mark Twain ever said this. But this quote is often attributed to him anyway.)

"Truth is stranger than fiction, but it is because Fiction is obliged to stick to possibilities; Truth isn't."—Mark Twain

(Okay, it is verified that Mark Twain actually said this. Phew!)

SCREEN STORY: THE BUSINESS OF "FAKE NEWS"

JC leads a pretty normal life. He's a dad and a husband who works hard to provide for his family. What's different about JC is what he used to do for work. He used to call himself a "fake news entrepreneur," or a person that creates and spreads false information.

Yes, you read that right. Some people make money by spreading fake stuff online.

At first, JC became a "fake news entrepreneur" to learn how false information spreads. He also hoped to expose the people spreading it. But he quickly realized he could make A LOT of money by creating and distributing fake news. Here's how he did it.

First, he built websites to look like actual news sites. These sites might include weather forecasts and real news stories to appear trustworthy. JC also made sure they had "real" sounding domain names, like NationalNews.com.

ALL DOGS ARE JUST BIG CATS
Ever wonder why your "dog" doesn't fetch the ball?

Study Links Blue Eyes To Being A Dinosaur
Check your children for scales NOW!

CAT BECOMES PRESIDENT OF USA!
Dill (5) is the youngest President ever.

Share this on social media!

He then wrote false news stories that he thought people might believe. He added these stories to his websites and shared them on social media. Many of these stories went viral, bringing people back to his ad-filled websites.

Cha-ching! JC made money as people saw and clicked on these ads.

JC no longer works in the fake news business. He now realizes that his work misled many people. By sharing his story, he hopes to illuminate the importance of **digital literacy**. After all, it's pretty easy to fool people online.

Fake news, **disinformation**, **misinformation**, flat-out lies . . . There is no shortage of phony stuff out there. Because the internet (and fingers) moves so fast, lies spread halfway around the world before the truth is uncovered. A study by the Massachusetts Institute of Technology found that false information spreads A LOT faster than truth. Yikes! (See the Weird Phone Trivia at the end of this chapter to learn how much faster.)

So how do people figure out what's true and what's fiction?

A good place to start is teaching people digital literacy, or the skills needed to succeed in our digital world. Digital literacy is not about finding information online (which is way too easy). It's about analyzing information to know whether it is reliable or not. And remember, just because people share something doesn't mean it is true.

 **DEFINITION:**

Digital literacy (noun): an individual's ability to find, evaluate, and communicate information on various digital platforms.

DEFINITION:

Disinformation (noun): false information that is spread on purpose to deceive.

DEFINITION:

Misinformation (noun): false or inaccurate information. (When people share misinformation, they might not realize the information is not true.)

 **WEIRD FACT:**

Posts and stories that trigger anger are shared more than any other type of information online. Jonah Berger, a professor at the Wharton School at the University of Pennsylvania, said, "Anger drives people to take action. It makes you feel fired up, which makes you more likely to pass things on."

TEST YOUR KNOWLEDGE—DISINFORMATION

Let's see how much you know about disinformation.

Please answer these true or false questions.

1. **True or False:** It's easy to spot **clickbait** and disinformation online because misleading and false stories look different.

2. **True or False:** "**Troll Farms**" are organizations that create and share offensive or false information to cause conflict or change public opinion.

3. **True or False:** FactCheck.org is a website focused on correcting false information.

Quiz Answers:

1. False. People who create and post false or misleading content make the information appear true.

2. True. "Troll Farms" actually exist! They pay people to post and spread information (often false) to influence others.

3. True. FactCheck.org is one of several sites focused on reducing the spread of false information.

📌 **DEFINITION:**

Clickbait (noun): the use of misleading or interesting titles and images online to get people to click on them. Yep, clickbait is fishing for your clicks. Don't bite these hooks!

REALITY CHECK—DETECTING DISINFORMATION

While disinformation often comes in the form of written text, it sometimes spreads as images or videos. Welcome to the world of **deepfakes**! Deepfakes are images and videos that have been edited to fool people into thinking they are real. For example, a video of the president may be altered to look and sound like the president is saying something they didn't actually say. Yikes!

YOU BE THE DETECTIVE

Let's test your eagle eye. Study the images below and decide whether each photo is real or a deepfake. A word of warning: deepfakes are hard to spot!

Image #1

Is this image real or a deepfake? _____

Image #2

Is this image real or a deepfake? _____

Answer: Got ya! Both are fake. Deepfakes often look so real it's difficult to tell they are not. So how can people tell what's real? See the healthy and safe habits at the end of this chapter for tips on how to analyze information you encounter online.

STRAIGHT TALK FROM TEENS:
HOW DO YOU DETECT DISINFORMATION?

Clickbait, deepfakes, fake news, oh my! With misinformation and disinformation everywhere, how can you discern truth from fiction? Teens shared how they detect phony stuff online. Feel free to add your insights too.

> If it seems too good, too weird, or too amazing to be true, I figure it is not true.

> Sometimes, fake stuff looks kind of funny. There are misspelled words, images look strange, and things just seem off.

> I try not to share things unless I'm really sure it is real.

> Whenever I see or read something that seems off, I fact-check the info on a site I trust.

Your thoughts:

_____

_____

_____

CRACK THE SECRET CODE—DISINFORMATION

Fill in the missing letters using the letter bank to complete each word. There are 16 missing letters in the sentence and 16 letters in the bank, so each letter should be used one time. If you get stuck, see the answer key in Chapter 10.

JU __T   __E__ AUSE   I__   __S   __HA__ED

O__LI__E   __OES   __OT   __A__E I__   __R__E.

Missing Letter Bank: N D R I C K S T N T U B S N M T

SUMMARY—DETECTING DISINFORMATION

False and misleading information is everywhere because of troll farms, fake news entrepreneurs, and folks sharing things they don't realize are false. Luckily, digital literacy helps you sleuth out the truth. Everyone plays a role in stopping the spread of disinformation. Before believing or sharing information online, be sure to follow the checklist below.

DETECTING DISINFORMATION—HEALTHY & SAFE HABITS CHECKLIST

	Background Check—Before you like or share a story or post, read more about it on a source you trust. Many false stories are shared because people do not take the time to read and analyze the information to make sure it is true.
	Check the Source—Only share information from trusted sources. To identify trustworthy sources, ask yourself the following questions: Who is the author? When was it written? Is it an opinion? Is the information based on facts?
	Think About the Evidence—Credible news stories usually include facts, quotes, and sources. Does the evidence add up?
	Don't Accept That Images or Videos Are Real—False news often uses real images or videos out of context or alters them. If it seems too strange to be true, it probably is.
	Ask for Help—If you are unsure about something you read or saw online, ask a trusted adult about it.

WEIRD PHONE TRIVIA #3

According to research by the Massachusetts Institute of Technology (MIT), false news stories are _____ percent more likely to be retweeted on Twitter than real news stories.

A. 25

B. 50

C. 70

D. 90

Answer: C. 70. Yep, false news is 70 percent more likely to be retweeted than true stories on Twitter. It also takes true stories six times longer to reach 1,500 people than it does for false stories. Mark Twain was spot on when he said, "Truth is more of a stranger than fiction."

CHAPTER 4

SOCIAL MEDIA—WELCOME TO DISNEYLAND

"Your eyes can deceive you. Don't trust them."
—Obi-Wan Kenobi

"Social media can deceive you. Don't trust it."
—Yours Truly :)

Before we dive in, it's important to note that the age requirement for most social media apps is 13+ as of the writing of this book. Just saying.

SCREEN STORY: LOST IN DISNEYLAND

When Kelsey's parents finally let her join social media, she jumped in with both thumbs. Within minutes, she followed friends and connected with classmates. She could see who was at the skate park and hanging out, who was cooking, and who was competing. She could even see what flavor cupcakes her friends were eating! Social media was like a door to the world that could be flung wide open with a few clicks and scrolls.

Social media felt like Disneyland. A beautiful, happy place that was open day and night with lots of different rides! So she started spending more time scrolling through her feeds and sharing selfies and posts. She checked her phone first thing in the morning, pretty much all day, and even late into the night.

But things started to change. When Kelsey was alone in her room, she found herself wishing she was having as much fun as everyone else, hoping her posts would get more likes, and wanting her selfies to look better. When she was feeling down, scrolling through her feeds often made her feel worse.

Wait! What happened to Disneyland? Social media is awesome—except when it's not. Social media helps people connect, share, and learn, but it has its downsides. Too much time on these apps can increase anxiety, decrease sleep and self-esteem, and more.

▦ Techy Tidbit:

Instagram started in 2010 and was purchased by Facebook in 2012 for $1,000,000,000. (That's a lot of zeros!) Fast forward several years, and Instagram has over a BILLION monthly users. The platform rakes in BILLIONS of dollars a year in profit by selling ads. Cha-ching!

TEST YOUR KNOWLEDGE—SOCIAL MEDIA

Let's see how firmly your feet (and phone) are planted in reality or lost in social media Disneyland. Please answer these true or false questions.

1. **True or False:** Social media is like real life, except on a little screen.

2. **True or False:** Software engineers design social media to encourage people to spend more time on the apps.

3. **True or False:** When you are bored or lonely, everyone else is having fun and posting on social media.

Quiz Answers:

1. False. People tend to share only their better moments and images on social media.

2. True. Software engineers design features like notifications, tagging, and feeds to increase the amount of time users spend on apps. The technical term for this is persuasive design (see Chapter 1).

3. False. Everyone feels bored and lonely sometimes.

REALITY CHECK—SOCIAL MEDIA

It's easy to confuse social media for real life, but it's not real life. Repeat: social media is NOT real life. It's a tool to help people connect, create, learn, and share. It's important to remember that much of what is posted on social media sometimes has more in common with Disneyland than real life. Here's how.

DISNEYLAND AND SOCIAL MEDIA VS. REAL LIFE

	Feelings	Faces	Places
Experiences at Disneyland	Mostly happy, happy, happy! 😌	Mostly smiling 🙂	Vibrant, fun (castles, roller coasters, **topiaries**, etc.)
Experiences Posted on Social Media	Mostly happy, happy, Happy! 😌	Mostly smiling 🐵 (and often altered by editing and filters)	Vibrant, fun (adventures, activities, and people doing fun stuff in cool places)
Experiences IRL (In Real Life)	Happy . . . plus bored, frustrated, sad, anxious, scared, embarrassed, and every other possible emotion 😌 😕 😵	Ordinary, including some bad hair days, pimples, and blank expressions staring into screens 😐 😴 🙃	A mix of ordinary and extraordinary (socks on the floor, unmade beds, breathtaking sunsets, etc.)

<u>Topiary</u> (noun): a shrub or tree cut into an ornamental shape. For example, a bush can be trimmed just right to look like a flying elephant.

Random Sketch Challenge

Imagine a shrub or tree near your home. Now, imagine this shrub or tree trimmed into a topiary the shape of your cell phone. Sketch below.

Lovely! Alright, back to social media.

STRAIGHT TALK FROM TEENS: WHAT ADVICE WOULD YOU GIVE SOMEONE WHO IS STARTING TO USE SOCIAL MEDIA?

Participating in social media comes with A LOT of choices and responsibilities, like deciding who to follow, what to post, and how often to check your feeds. Several teens shared advice on how to use social media in positive ways and how to avoid common pitfalls. Feel free to add your insights too!

Make sure your social media accounts are private. Only let people follow you if you know them and are comfortable with them following you.

Do not judge yourself or others by likes or followers. This has NOTHING to do with who you or they are as people.

Be very aware that when you post photos about a party or event, the post will be seen by the friends you did not invite. Before posting, ask yourself, 'Do I really need to post this?'

Use social media to connect with friends and to express yourself. Don't use it to be rude or harm others. And if you need help, reaching out to a friend or adult is better than **sadfishing**.

Your advice:

_____

_____

_____

📌 DEFINITION:

<u>Sadfishing</u> (noun): when a person posts personal struggles online to get support or sympathy. CAUTION: This may backfire and attract trolls or bullying! If you are struggling, talk directly to a trusted adult or friend to get the support you need.

SCREEN STORY: HOW JOSHUA USED SOCIAL MEDIA TO FEED THE HUNGRY

When Joshua was four years old, he met a homeless man. The man's lack of food and shelter left an ache in Joshua's heart that he couldn't ignore. Luckily, Joshua had a $20 bill and an idea. With the help of his parents, he used his money to buy food for homeless families.

Joshua wanted to help more people, so he and his parents organized a local fundraiser and shared it on their social media accounts. Joshua's generosity inspired others to donate food and money, which helped Joshua feed hundreds of struggling families. A few months later, Joshua and his parents expanded their charitable efforts and created Joshua's Heart Foundation in his hometown of Miami, Florida. By the time he was seven years old, the organization was feeding thousands of families every month.

Joshua, now in his twenties, is still hard at work. He uses his website, JoshuasHeart.org, and social media to encourage people to volunteer and donate food and money to feed people in need. To date, Joshua's Heart Foundation has served 5 million meals, raised over $3 million, and assisted more than 600,000 individuals.

With the help of his family, a big dose of inspiration, and the effective use of social media, Joshua is working to stamp out hunger in his community. Social media is a powerful tool to connect with and inspire others and to bring about change. Joshua did just that, making real life a bit more like Disneyland.

CRACK THE SECRET CODE—SOCIAL MEDIA

Use the table below to crack the Morse code message. To get you started, the first word has been decoded for you. If you get stuck, see the answer key in Chapter 10.

A ·−	B −···	C −·−·
D −··	E ·	F ··−·
G −−·	H ····	I ··
J ·−−−	K −·−	L ·−··
M −−	N −·	O −−−
P ·−−·	Q −−·−	R ·−·
S ···	T −	U ··−
V ···−	W ·−−	X −··−
Y −·−−	Z −−··	

··−/···/·/ .... USE

···/−−−/−·−·/··/·−/·−··/ ....

−−/·/−··/··/·−/ ....

−/−−−/ ....

−−/·−/−·−/·/ ....

−/····/·/ ....

·−−/−−−/·−·/·−··/−··/ ....

−···/·/−/−/·/·−·/ ....

STRAIGHT TALK FROM TEENS:
HOW TO USE SOCIAL MEDIA FOR GOOD

Social media is a tool to connect with others, express yourself, and learn new things. Like spray paint, submarines, and hot sauce, social media can be a force for good or not so good. Here's how some teens use social media to make a positive impact:

> I know a lot of teens are self-conscious about how they look, what they say, and what they do. So when people put themselves out there, I always send positive comments.

> I get educated on world issues I care about and do what I can to raise awareness so my friends and family understand them too.

> I use my phone to learn new things and communicate with friends.

> I use social media to post cool photos because I love photography.

What are some ways you might use social media as a force for good?

_____

_____

_____

SUMMARY—SOCIAL MEDIA

In several studies, researchers found that the more hours a day teens use social media, the more likely they are to feel sad or depressed. Yikes! If you participate in social media, be sure to spend time with people in-person and do offline things you enjoy. Here's a checklist you can follow to keep your social media habits healthy and safe.

SOCIAL MEDIA—HEALTHY & SAFE HABITS CHECKLIST

	Stay Balanced—Spend time offline doing activities you enjoy (sports, music, art, or outdoor activities).
	Be Kind—Avoid harsh posts and criticizing others online. Have tough conversations face-to-face. Texts and DMs are easily misunderstood.

Set Limits—Set daily screen time limits and turn off notifications.
Stay Private—Use a nickname for your profiles instead of your real name and keep your accounts private. Never share your full name, your address, your location, or any personal information with people you meet online.
Be You—Never pretend to be someone you are not.
Think Before You Post—Remember that your posts are out there for everyone to see, save, and share! Do not share inappropriate pictures or posts.
Friends Only—Some people use social media to stalk people, steal information, or cause harm. Only accept friend requests from people you know (see Chapter 7).
Ask for Help—If you see something concerning or experience teasing or harassment, talk to an adult right away!

WEIRD PHONE TRIVIA #4

What medical issue has become more prevalent as people spend more time staring down at their phones?

  A. Blurry vision

  B. Sore wrists

  C. Text neck

  D. Thumb strain

Answer: C. Text neck. In recent years, bone growths at the base of the neck (also known as enlarged external occipital protuberance) have been showing up more frequently on the X-rays of people aged eighteen to thirty. This is likely caused by a bent neck posture due to excessive handheld technology use.

CHAPTER 5

FOMO, FOJI, AND TEXT SLANG GALORE

"Just because something works doesn't mean it cannot be improved."—Shuri, Princess of Wakanda

"Just because texts and social media connect people, doesn't mean people feel connected."—Yours Truly :)

SCREEN STORY: A ONE-WEEK SOCIAL MEDIA BAN

To understand the effect of social media on their lives, nine students in England decided to give up social media for one week. No checking their feeds, no posting, and no responding to messages from friends. Zip!

This week-long social media ban was not easy for these teens. To document their experience, they recorded daily vlogs (video blogs). Here's what some participants shared:

Day 1: It's the first day, and I'm unsure of what I should replace the time I spend on social media with.

Day 3: This is quite hard. I don't know what to do with my laptop. There's nothing to do anymore.

Day 5: Since I'm not checking my accounts, I think I'm missing out on things.

Day 7: The weekend was challenging. I wondered what my friends were doing.

The social media ban grew more difficult for the students as each day passed. They experienced intense emotions, like boredom, loneliness, and fear. Not to mention stress! Their discomfort was so intense that only three students remained on day seven. The six students who did not complete the challenge shared similar reasons for dropping out:

It was nice to get more free time, but I didn't know what to do with the free time.

By not checking my accounts, I felt like I was missing out on something.

Since many teens use social media to socialize and connect with friends, it makes sense that they feel intense emotions, like anxiety and fear, when they are disconnected. Welcome to the world of **FOMO**!

 DEFINITION:

FOMO (noun): An acronym for the "fear of missing out" or anxiety stemming from the belief that others might be having fun without you or that you are missing out on information, experiences, or things that could make your life better. FOMO also involves envy that others are living a better life.

TEST YOUR KNOWLEDGE—TEXT SLANG

FOMO is just the tip of the iceberg regarding social media and text slang. Some acronyms, like FOMO, explain feelings and behaviors. Others simplify phrases, so you don't have to type so much. Do you know the text slang below?

1. What is FOJI?

_____

_____

_____

2. What is JOMO?

_____

_____

_____

3. What is FOMO?

_____

_____

_____

Quiz Answers:

1. "Fear of joining in" because you are unsure of what to post or are afraid others will not like or comment on your photos.

2. "Joy of missing out" or taking pleasure in not having to be doing what everyone else is doing—the opposite of FOMO.

3. "Fear of missing out." Thought we better include at least one easy question! You're welcome.

>  **WEIRD FACT:**
>
> The first cell phone call was made on April 3, 1973, by Motorola engineer Martin Cooper in New York City. This phone looked nothing like today's sleek devices. It resembled a brick with buttons and an antenna!

>  **WEIRD FACT:**
>
> The first text message was transmitted on December 3, 1992. Engineer Neil Papworth typed "Merry Christmas" on a computer and sent the message to the cellphone of Richard Jarvis.

REALITY CHECK—FOMO

FOMO existed well before social media. Let's face it: everyone feels left out sometimes or wishes they were experiencing what others are experiencing. Welcome to life as a human being.

However, with the invention of social media, FOMO is much more common. In just a few clicks, you see photos of your friends enjoying fun times without you. You see clothes you wish you had and lives that seem better than yours. In today's tech-obsessed world, it's easy to compare your life to the highlights others post about theirs.

If you find yourself lost in FOMO, remember, you are not alone. Feelings of sadness, loneliness, and jealousy are part of the human experience even though they are not comfortable or fun. To navigate FOMO and uncomfortable emotions, try to do something you enjoy. Maybe play some music, connect with a friend, or get outside. Or you could reread this book. (Sorry, I couldn't resist :)

BEGINNER LEVEL—MATCH THE TEXT SLANG

Feeling FOMO or FOJI? It could be time to connect with a friend or do something fun. This next activity will help you brush up on your texting skills.

Match the abbreviations in the left column with their meaning on the right to test your knowledge of text phrases. GL! (Good luck!)

1.	BRB	I know, right
2.	HBD	Not much
3.	SMH	I don't care
4.	NBD	What about you?
5.	NM	Never mind
6.	IKR	How about you?
7.	GTR	I don't know
8.	OMW	Be right back

9. HBU	Shaking my head
10. IDC	Got to run
11. NVM	Rolling on the floor laughing
12. DYK	No big deal
13. WBU	Happy birthday
14. IDK	Did you know
15. ROFL	On my way

Answers: 1. Be right back 2. Happy birthday 3. Shaking my head 4. No big deal 5. Not much 6. I know, right 7. Got to run 8. On my way 9. How about you? 10. I don't care 11. Nevermind 12. Did you know 13. What about you? 14. I don't know 15. Rolling on the floor laughing

ADVANCED LEVEL—FILL-IN-THE-BLANK TEXT SLANG

Congratulations! You are ready to advance to the next level. Read the text slang below and write what it means in the right column. The first one has been done for you. YGT! (You got this!)

1. DM	Direct Message
2. TTYL	
3. MTFBWY	
4. TBH	
5. IMHO	
6. HTH	

7. FYI	
8. LMK	
9. JK	
10. IRL	

Answers–Advanced Level: 1. Direct message 2. Talk to you later 3. May the Force be with you 4. To be honest 5. In my humble opinion 6. Here to help OR happy to help 7. For your information 8. Let me know 9. Just kidding 10. In real life

SUPER ADVANCED LEVEL—CREATE YOUR OWN TEXT SLANG

Nice work! Time to invent some new text slang. Read each scenario below and create your own acronym or abbreviation that fits the situation. MTFBWY.

Scenario 1: You and your classmates misunderstood the instructions in science lab and exploded your sample of sulfur. The classroom now reeks of rotten eggs. You text your friend: _____

_____

Scenario 2: Your friend has a crush on someone, and you just heard that this person likes your friend too. You text your friend: _____

_____

STRAIGHT TALK FROM TEENS:
HOW DO YOU DEAL WITH FOMO?

Humans share the need to feel acceptance and belonging, especially in the preteen and teen years. Humans also tend to compare themselves to others. This means everyone experiences FOMO from time to time. Here's how some teens say they deal with FOMO. Feel free to add your insights too!

> TBH, I hate it when I see friends posting about things I wasn't included in. It's really hard. At these times, I usually reach out to another friend to get my mind off it.

> I try to stay connected to my close friends so I feel like I'm part of the group.

> I try not to take it personally. Everybody is not always involved or included in everything.

> I remind myself that many of the selfies and photos on social media are edited with filters. They are not real.

Your thoughts:

_____

_____

_____

CRACK THE SECRET CODE—FOMO

Decipher the text slang below to unlock the secret code. This message will help you combat FOMO. See the answer key in Chapter 10 if you get stuck.

IMHO, ...

UR   ....

GR8   ....

IRL.   ....

MTFBWY!   ....

SUMMARY—FOMO

FOMO is a real and familiar feeling for people of all ages. It takes a toll on moods and self-esteem. Remember, too much time on social media increases the chances of feeling anxiety, so be sure to balance your time on screens with time off screens. The following habits will help you navigate uncomfortable emotions prompted by screen time.

FOMO–HEALTHY & SAFE HABITS CHECKLIST

	Change Your Focus—When you find yourself lost in FOMO, shift your focus to the cool things in your life and what you are grateful for.
	Connect with a Friend or Family—Feelings of loneliness or exclusion are your brain's way of telling you to reach out and connect with someone. Text a friend, talk to a trusted adult, or make plans to meet up with a classmate.
	Change Your Feed—Try to notice what posts and apps make you feel down. Change your feed to show you less of those posts and more of what inspires you.
	Avoid Jumping to Conclusions—If you notice you were not included in something, avoid jumping to conclusions about why. There could be all sorts of reasons.
	Ask for Help—If lonely or sad feelings persist, it might be time to reach out to a trusted adult. We all need a little help from time to time.

WEIRD PHONE TRIVIA #5

Between 2011 and 2017, five times more people died while taking selfies than _____ .

A. in shark attacks

B. in motorcycle accidents

C. by lightning strikes

D. while skydiving

Answer: A. in shark attacks. Between October 2011 and November 2017, at least 259 people died taking selfies around the globe, according to the Journal of Family Medicine and Primary Care. Fifty people were killed by sharks during the same period.

CHAPTER 6:

ZOMBIE LAND–IS TECH ADDICTION A THING?

"In a dark place we find ourselves, and a little more knowledge lights our way." **—Yoda**

"In a dark place we may find ourselves if only tech lights our way." **—Yours Truly :)**

SCREEN STORY: KELLY'S PHONE OBSESSION

Kelly was a happy kid and a strong student, but that changed when she got her first phone. She spent so much time on her phone that she rarely came out of her bedroom. Her grades sank as her obsession grew.

To help Kelly, her parents tried to limit her screen time, but Kelly became defiant. She started sneaking on her phone at all hours of the night. When Kelly's grades hit rock bottom, her parents told her she could no longer have her phone at night. Kelly refused. She screamed and threw things. Her violent behavior frightened her parents so much that they called the police. Her parents hardly recognized their daughter. They feared for her health and safety.

Kelly's family started seeing a counselor, who said Kelly was suffering from depression and an obsession with her phone. Even though Kelly claimed that only the time she spent on her phone made her happy, it was clear to those who loved her that she was struggling even when she was on her phone.

After months of family counseling, Kelly started to feel better. She got back into activities she enjoyed. Her grades and her relationship with her parents improved. Her family agreed on rules to keep Kelly's screen time at healthy levels. It was a difficult journey, but Kelly and her parents learned a lot about the power of technology and the importance of balancing time on and off screens.

Many parents are worried that their kids are "addicted" to their phones. Teens sometimes use the word "addicted" to describe their behavior **TOO**. In a survey by Common Sense Media, half of the teen participants said they felt like they were addicted to their phones. Three-quarters of them said they felt they needed to respond to texts, social media posts, and other notifications immediately.

So is tech addiction really a thing?

TEST YOUR KNOWLEDGE—TECH ADDICTION

Let's see how **MUCH** you know about **TECH** "addiction." Please answer these true or false questions.

1. **True or False:** A lot of what kids do online is healthy.

2. **True or False:** Research finds that heavy social media use or gaming is not a risk factor for anxiety and depression.

3. **True or False:** If kids have enough time for all of the important activities in their lives, such as sleeping, eating, exercising, and doing schoolwork, the amount of time they spend on screens is probably okay.

Quiz Answers:

1. True. Many of the things kids do on devices are activities that have been done offline in the past, such

as socializing with friends, exploring interests, listening to music, doing schoolwork, and watching movies.

2. False. There **IS** evidence that intense social media use correlates with increased anxiety and depression as teens, especially girls, compare themselves to their peers and worry about missing out. Research also shows that excessive gaming is connected with negative mental health issues.

3. True. Spending a lot of time online becomes a problem when it interferes with a person's ability to lead a healthy life. For instance, if someone is **NOT** sleeping, eating, or exercising enough, it may be a sign of **problematic internet use** or a **gaming disorder**.

📌 DEFINITION:

Problematic internet use (PIU) (noun): an inability to control one's use of the internet, which leads to negative consequences in daily life.

📌 DEFINITION:

Gaming disorder (noun): when a person has trouble controlling the amount of time they spend playing video games. They prioritize gaming over other activities and experience negative effects from their gaming behaviors.

According to the World Health Organization, a person who has a gaming disorder will show the following characteristics for at least 12 months:

· lacking control over their gaming habits

· prioritizing gaming over other interests and activities

· continuing gaming despite its negative consequences

So yeah, technology can negatively impact kids if they spend so much time on screens they skimp on eating, getting **A GOOD** night's sleep, doing homework, or spending time with friends and family. If you stumble upon someone with sluggish movements, scrappy clothes, and bloodshot eyes who can't stop staring at their phone, they may be struggling with PIU. Or maybe it's a **zombie**?!

When someone is focused on screens to the point of isolation, they may be experiencing other mental health struggles as well. Sometimes people disappear into screens because they feel anxious or depressed or they have a learning difference.

But it's important to remember that many **THING**s kids do online are normal and healthy. In the dark ages, when your parents were young, kids socialized in person, listened to music on **boom boxes**, played board games, and went to the movies. Now, much of this happens on devices. No wonder everyone seems to be staring at their screens.

> 📌 **DEFINITION:**
>
> <u>Boom box</u> (noun): a portable sound system typically including a radio and a cassette or CD player.

> 📌 **DEFINITION:**
>
> <u>Zombie</u> (noun): a dead body that has been brought back to life by a supernatural force, or someone who acts in a mechanical or apathetic way.

> 👽 **WEIRD FACT:**
>
> Kids and teens in China are barred from online gaming on school days and are limited to one hour a day on weekends and holidays.

REALITY CHECK—TECH ADDICTION

So, how much screen time is too much? How do we know when video watching, gaming, or social media use spikes to unhealthy levels? Review the habits below and check whether you think each person shows healthy or unhealthy screen habits.

1. JD plays video games for more hours than he sleeps. He plays so late into the night he has a hard time getting up for school and staying awake in class.

   ☐ Healthy   ☐ Unhealthy

2. Davana can't stop checking social media. She watches how many likes her posts get compared to others. She takes selfies and edits her pictures to perfection. Her time on social media makes her feel bad about herself.

☐ Healthy   ☐ Unhealthy

3. Charlie watches YouTube videos every night to learn how to play the guitar. It's taken a lot of time to learn, but he has found excellent teachers and resources online.

☐ Healthy   ☐ Unhealthy

4. Olin spends most of his time in bed watching videos and scrolling social media. He hardly showers and has lost interest in going to school.

☐ Healthy   ☐ Unhealthy

5. Amal loves texting friends and connecting on social media. She knows it takes courage for many girls to share selfies and posts, so she supports her peers by leaving positive comments.

☐ Healthy   ☐ Unhealthy

If you checked #1, #2, and #4 as unhealthy, you are correct. It appears that these screen habits have dipped into the zombie zone and maybe even **nomophobia**. JD, Davana, and Olin's screen time is harming their daily lives. They may also be struggling with their mental health and may need support from a trusted adult or counselor.

STRAIGHT TALK FROM TEENS: HOW DO YOU KEEP FROM BECOMING ADDICTED TO YOUR PHONE?

As you learned in Chapter 1, **persuasive design** makes it easy to keep playing, scrolling, and staring at devices. Phones, apps, and technology are designed to keep people drooling like zombies. Before you know it, hours have passed, and you realize you forgot to eat, do homework, and sleep. Here's how some teens combat phone addiction. Feel free to add your insights too!

> I figured out that it takes me twice as long to do my homework if I am also checking texts and watching videos. Now I put my phone away until I get my homework done.

> It's sad to me that people no longer live life for themselves. It's more like they do things for a photo op for social media. I try to live IRL.

I got into a bad habit of sleeping with my phone in my room. Having it near my bed made me want to keep checking for new messages. I sleep a lot better now that my phone is out of the room.

Your thoughts:

SCREEN STORY: TRISTAN'S CRUSADE TO IMPROVE BIG TECH

Tristan Harris studied computer science at Stanford University before starting a job at Google. As Tristan learned more about Google's business operations, he became more and more concerned about how tech companies negatively shape people's lives. He said, "Never before in history have a handful of technology designers working at tech companies influenced how a billion people spend their attention."

To improve technology for the common good of people, Tristan founded the Center for Humane Technology. This organization studies how tech platforms use their power and how they can operate more ethically.

Tristan is on a global mission to help big tech companies prioritize people over profit. He meets with world leaders, executives, and members of the US Congress to share his findings and inspire change. He has mobilized millions of people worldwide who support making technology work for the common good.

Tristan was named in *TIME* magazine's "100 Next Leaders Shaping the Future" and *Rolling Stone* magazine's "25 People Shaping the World."

Indeed, Tristan's efforts are shaping technology for a better future. Thanks to his work and to new laws, some tech companies are beginning to consider people's well-being when designing technology. But there is still work to be done. In the meantime, it's up to us to watch our screen habits to avoid entering zombie land.

WEIRD FACT:

Dopamine is a type of neurotransmitter that plays a role in how we feel pleasure. Hearing the ding of a new message, receiving "likes," or reaching a new game level all trigger the release of dopamine. As a result, some people can become obsessed with online pleasure-seeking experiences, like playing video games or checking social media.

Hmmm, that explains why it feels good when our phone bings with a new message!

CRACK THE SECRET CODE—TECH ADDICTION

Scan this chapter to find eight words that are CAPITALIZED, underlined, and **bolded**. In order of appearance, write the words below to reveal the secret code. The first word has been added for you to get you started. If you get stuck, see the answer key in Chapter 10.

TOO

SUMMARY—TECH ADDICTION

Well, it turns out the old saying is true. "Too much of a good thing" is not good. Too much candy makes you feel sick. Too much exercise is hard on the body. And too much screen time can make someone a tech zombie. Yikes! Studies find that too much tech time is not good for your physical or mental health. Here's a checklist to help you keep your screen time in the healthy zone.

TECH ADDICTION—HEALTHY & SAFE HABITS CHECKLIST

	Set Limits—Set daily screen time limits and turn off notifications.
	Stay Balanced—Spend time offline doing activities you enjoy (sports, music, art, or outdoor activities).
	Keep Devices Out of Your Bedroom at Night—Kids need an average of 9-11 hours of uninterrupted sleep a night to stay healthy! Leave your phone in a different room when you're ready for bed.
	Turn Off Notifications—Turn off notifications on apps that distract you from doing other things you could or should be doing.
	Ask for Help—If your screen habits are negatively impacting your life, it's time to reach out to a trusted adult.

WEIRD PHONE TRIVIA #6

The AAA Foundation for Traffic Safety conducted a study about texting and driving. They found that texting while driving _____ the chances for a car accident.

    A. doubles

    B. reduces

    C. stops

    D. quadruples

Answer: A. doubles. In the five seconds people spend reading or writing a text message, they're leaving themselves wide open to an accident. Since a car can travel the distance of a football field in five seconds, it makes sense that texting while driving doubles the risk for a car wreck.

CHAPTER 7

CREEPY PEOPLE—STRANGER DANGER ONLINE

"If no one else will defend the world, then I must."
—Wonder Woman

"No one else can fully protect you online, so you must."
—Yours Truly :)

SCREEN STORY: FAKE PROFILES AND STRANGER DANGER

A YouTube **influencer** with over a million subscribers used his platform to remind kids and parents about stranger danger online. To prove a point, he made a fake social media profile of a 15-year-old boy. He then friend requested three girls, ages 12, 13, and 14. (He secretly asked their parents' permission first, letting them know about his plan.)

Next, he messaged the girls and showered them with compliments using the fake profile. He said things like "You are so pretty" and "I'd love to get to know you." A few days later, he invited each one to meet him in real life.

USER PROFILE
LUKE
AGE: 15
NEW YORK
message

you are so pretty

The parents in the experiment believed their daughters would never agree to meet a stranger they met online. What happened surprised them.

Each girl agreed to meet the influencer in person. One girl met him at a park. Another invited him to her house after her parents were asleep. And the third snuck out of her house and got into his car.

Imagine the girls' surprise when instead of meeting a 15-year-old boy, they met the terrified and disappointed gaze of their parents. When the shock passed, the influencer reminded the girls of the dangerous consequences of their decision. Luckily, this story ended with an important lesson rather than in tragedy.

Most people are kind. But unfortunately, creepy people are out there, and they use technology to stalk and harm others. It's easy for someone to hide their identity online.

With a few fake photos and posts, a stranger can pretend to be someone or something they're not. So that friend request from a teenager might be a 47-year-old. Yikes!

🖈 **DEFINITION:**

<u>Influencer</u> (noun): a person who inspires or guides the actions of others, or a person who can generate interest in something (such as a product) by posting about it on social media.

TEST YOUR KNOWLEDGE— STRANGER DANGER ONLINE

Let's see how much you know about stranger danger online. Please answer these true or false questions.

1. **True or False:** It's safe to open links and files shared with you by direct message, email, or text.

2. **True or False:** When someone you met online asks you personal questions, sends inappropriate images, or wants to meet in person, it's essential to report this behavior to a trusted adult.

3. **True or False:** The Federal Trade Commission (FTC) receives over 2 million reports of fraud a year, with the most common category being imposter scams, followed by online shopping scams.

Quiz Answers:

1. False. Computer hackers often send links and files to spread viruses and inappropriate content or to trick you into giving away personal information. If you don't know the sender, don't click or open the link.

2. True. Report this behavior to a trusted adult. Be sure to keep personal information, such as your full name, address, phone number, school, and location, private.

3. True. In 2021, the FTC received 2.8 million reports of fraud by customers.

▦ TECHY TIDBIT:

Any link you receive in an email, direct message, or text should be looked at with a suspicious eye. If you don't know the sender, don't click on the link! If you do know the sender, make sure they did indeed send it before you click on it. Criminals often create fake accounts and pretend to be someone you know. This is a common **phishing** trick. Don't take the bait.

Phishing (noun, pronounced /fi-shing/): a common trick used by identity thieves to gain someone's personal information. This crime involves sending emails or using websites that appear real and asking people to confirm personal information, such as bank account numbers, passwords, birth dates, or addresses.

REALITY CHECK—STRANGER DANGER ONLINE

Now that you're creeped out, let's explore how to stay safe online. Luckily there are ways to avoid hackers and online villains. And the good news is, no superhero cape is required to outsmart them. You can protect yourself and be your own superhero by being careful about what you click on and who you follow and talk to online.

RED LIGHT–GREEN LIGHT GAME

Let's put your stranger danger superpowers to work! Read the online scenarios below and check either RED LIGHT or GREEN LIGHT. RED LIGHT means the scenario is fishy (or phishy) and potentially dangerous, so you should stop and get help from a trusted adult. GREEN LIGHT means everything is a-okay, so you can go ahead without any worries.

SCENARIO	RED LIGHT (STOP!)	GREEN LIGHT (GO!)
1. You get a direct message on social media from somebody new. They ask you questions like "How old are you? Where do you live? Can you send me a selfie?" **What do you do?**		
2. In a private group chat, you and your friends talk about movies. Your friend shares a video clip from your favorite movie. **Do you watch the video?**		
3. You get a text from someone you don't know. It includes a weblink. **Do you click on the link to see what it is?**		
4. Joe Shmoe sends you a friend request on social media. You have no idea who this person is, but you see that some of your friends have friended him. **Do you accept this friend request?**		

If you checked RED LIGHT for scenarios #1, #3, and #4, phew! Good work. Those scenarios are pretty sketchy. With so many posts, texts, and DMs, it's sometimes hard to know when a situation is dangerous or safe. If a post, text, or DM makes you uncomfortable, seems too good to be true, or is just plain weird, consider it a RED LIGHT. When a stranger contacts you online, **don't click, don't respond, and check with an adult**. In the digital world, it's better to be safe than sorry.

👽 **WEIRD FACT:**

Social media companies remove billions (yes, billions) of fake accounts, but as soon as one is removed, another is created.

STRAIGHT TALK FROM TEENS: HOW DO YOU DEAL WITH STRANGER DANGER AND STAY SAFE ONLINE?

Stranger danger is real and, well, for lack of a better word, dangerous. Here's how some teens stay safe online. Feel free to add your insights too!

> Sometimes I get texts or DMs from people I don't know with web links. I immediately delete and block them.

My social media accounts are private and under a nickname instead of my real name. This gives me more privacy and means only people I know see my posts.

I used to accept friend requests from friends of friends, even if I didn't know them. This got weird, so now I only accept friend requests from people I know and like.

When playing video games, I remember that the person on the other side of the screen could be anyone and not who they say they are. Sometimes I exit the game if things get strange.

Your thoughts:

_____

_____

_____

SCREEN STORY: THE SUPERHEROES FIGHTING CYBERCRIME

Cybercrime grows every year. Criminals target companies and people to steal data, money, and more. Thankfully, there are superheroes fighting cybercrime to make the world safer.

The World Economic Forum's Partnership Against Cybercrime is a global network of organizations working to slow cybercrime. Just like Marvel superheroes, these governments, law enforcement agencies, and organizations around the world work together to arrest cybercriminals and foil their dastardly schemes.

The fight against cybercrime is far from over and may never end. But the more people work together to stop cybercrime, the more chances we have to stop it in its tracks.

📌 **DEFINITION:**

<u>Cybercrime</u> (noun): also called computer crime, the use of a computer and the internet to further illegal ends, such as committing fraud, stealing identities, and violating privacy.

CRACK THE SECRET CODE—
STRANGER DANGER ONLINE

Rearrange the words below to complete the sentence about stranger danger online. Hint: This sentence appeared earlier in this chapter.

an	adult	check	click
respond	with	don't	don't

When a stranger contacts you online, _____

_____ , _____ _____ ,

and _____ _____ _____

_____ .

SUMMARY—STRANGER DANGER ONLINE

Well, cybercriminals and scary people are lurking out there, especially online. Creepy! But there are things you can do to hone your stranger danger superpowers. Keep yourself safe by following the checklist below.

	Keep Your Profiles Private—This can prevent strangers from following you online.
	Only Accept Friend Requests from People You Know—Even if you have mutual friends, do not accept friend requests from strangers.
	Remember That It's Easy for People to Pretend to Be Someone Else Online—Photos, profiles, posts, and messages can easily be faked.
	Never Share Personal Information—Keep your name, address, phone number, birthday, social security number, passwords, parents' information, and school name private.
	Do Not Respond to Messages or Texts from Unknown Senders—Do not open links or files in messages from strangers as they often include viruses or inappropriate content.
	Get Help—Tell an adult immediately if someone sends you inappropriate photos, asks you to meet, or makes you uncomfortable. NEVER meet a person you met online in real life.

WEIRD PHONE TRIVIA #7

Bluetooth is the short-range wireless connection between mobile phones, computers, and devices. For example, you use Bluetooth to play music from your phone on a wireless speaker.

Where did Bluetooth technology get its name?

A. A frozen tooth

B. A Viking

C. A relative of Bigfoot

D. None of the above

Answer: B. A Viking. Bluetooth got its name from Viking King Harald "Bluetooth" Gormsson, who is known for uniting Denmark and Norway in 958 AD. His dead tooth, a dark blue color, earned him his nickname.

CHAPTER 8:

CYBERBULLYING AND DIGITAL DRAMA, UGH

"When you decide not to be afraid, you can find friends in super unexpected places." —Ms. Marvel

"When you choose to be kind, you can find friends in super unexpected places." —Yours Truly :)

SCREEN STORY: AN ANGRY POST GONE WRONG

The 9th graders in Sophia's school were having a big party. Unfortunately, Sophia had other plans that night. Upset that everyone was having fun without her, she posted a rude comment on social media. Her post made fun of some girls at the party, making it sound like Sophia didn't want to go and hang out with them.

The post went unnoticed until someone found and shared it a month later. Sophia's comments caused quite a stir, so she apologized to make things right.

Things settled down for a while until Sophia posted a selfie. Several people replied with mean comments. Feeling hurt, Sophia reached out to the girl who posted first. The girl responded, "It's a joke. We are just having fun."

The harsh posts about Sophia continued and grew into threats. People from other schools even chimed in. Sophia's friends tried to comfort her, but they did not defend her. Sophia felt scared and alone.

Not sure what else to do, she told her parents what was happening. Her mom contacted the school counselor, who shared the school's code of conduct policy. The counselor confirmed that the behavior directed at Sophia was indeed **cyberbullying**.

The school principal contacted the kids and families involved. The students blamed Sophia and her post about the party for starting the problem. The principal explained that Sophia made a mistake with her post, but it was not okay for others to cyberbully in response.

Weeks later, Sophia met with one of the girls involved. The girl apologized for her rude comments. They decided to move forward and do their best to spread kindness on social media from then on.

Sophia learned a lot from this experience. She learned to be careful about what she posts, especially when she feels angry or upset. She also learned that nobody deserves to be treated the way she was treated and that it's important to get help if you experience cyberbullying.

....

Everyone's seen or heard about bullying and social drama in real life. With the growth of technology, these behaviors shifted online. Unfortunately, people sometimes share things on devices that they would never say to someone face-to-face. They forget that a human being is behind every screen. Welcome to the world of cyberbullying and **digital drama**. Ugh. So what is cyberbullying, exactly? And what is digital drama? Sometimes it's hard to know the difference, so let's dive into some definitions.

📌 DEFINITION:

Cyberbullying (noun): the use of technology to harass, threaten, embarrass, or target another person. Cyberbullying has four characteristics: 1. It happens online. 2. It's done on purpose. 3. It's repeated. 4. It's harmful.

DEFINITION:

Digital Drama (noun): misunderstandings, arguments, and mean comments that occur between friends or acquaintances online. Digital drama falls short of cyberbullying because it may not be repeated and both sides may be involved.

TEST YOUR KNOWLEDGE—CYBERBULLYING

Let's see how much you know about cyberbullying. Please answer these true or false questions.

1. **True or False:** Cyberbullying often happens on apps or websites that allow people to make anonymous posts.

2. **True or False:** Cyberbullying does not happen on gaming sites.

3. **True or False:** Cyberbullying often goes unreported even when there are witnesses.

Quiz Answers:

1. True. Apps and websites that allow people to post things anonymously are hotspots for cyberbullying.

2. False. Chat features in gaming allow people to send inappropriate and cruel messages.

3. True. Both witnesses and targets of cyberbullying may be hesitant to report it. They may be embarrassed, afraid, or worried that bullying will increase if they draw attention to it.

This is not fun stuff! Imagine being on the receiving end of repeated, harsh comments online. Nobody deserves to be treated this way. Cyberbullying is harmful and needs to stop.

Digital drama feels terrible too; it's hurtful to those involved even though it falls short of cyberbullying. Maybe it's not repeated. Or perhaps both sides are attacking each other. For example, two kids arguing and insulting each other on social media is digital drama. This needs to stop too!

But even though cyberbullying and digital drama are alive and well online, you can help stop these behaviors in their tracks. As a **digital citizen**, you play an important role in protecting yourself online, reporting abusive comments, and being kind. When you practice good digital citizenship, you make the internet a better place!

📌 **DEFINITION:**

Digital Citizen (noun): a person who develops the skills and knowledge to effectively use the internet and other digital technology, especially in order to participate responsibly in social and civic activities.

REALITY CHECK—CYBERBULLYING & DIGITAL DRAMA

Cyberbullying and digital drama are nasty stuff! Why can't people just be nice?!

Even though you can't control others' actions, you can practice digital citizenship and control what YOU post online. What you post, share, and report to adults and online platforms plays a role in making the internet a friendlier and safer place to hang out.

RED LIGHT–GREEN LIGHT (ADVANCED LEVEL)

Last chapter we played Red Light, Green Light to tell the difference between safe and unsafe situations online. Let's play again—but at an advanced level! Grab a red and green pencil or marker. Read each scenario below and decide whether it is cyberbullying or digital drama (RED LIGHT) or digital citizenship (GREEN LIGHT). Some scenarios might be both RED and GREEN. The first scenario has been done for you. Ready, set, go!

RED LIGHT: Cyberbullying or Digital Drama		GREEN LIGHT: Good Digital Citizenship
	Someone posts insults and rumors about the volleyball team on a fake social media account.	
	JD messaged "PLEASE STOP!" to some kids who were humiliating Carlos on Snapchat. He checked in with Carlos later to be sure he was doing ok.	

	Katie and Sam are fighting on social media, calling each other names and making threats. Other kids are getting involved and taking sides.	
	Someone took a photo of Zack changing in the locker room and posted it anonymously.	
	When Malia sees two girls insulting each other online, she encourages them to take it offline and work it out face-to-face.	

Answer: All of these scenarios include digital drama or cyberbullying (RED LIGHT), but the actions of two bystanders, JD and Malia, also include good digital citizenship (GREEN LIGHT).

 **WEIRD FACT:**

Wikipedia's mission is to make knowledge freely available to anyone with access to the internet. However, anyone with the internet can also sign up and edit Wikipedia's pages, including trolls, cyberbullies, and spreaders of disinformation. That's where Wikipedia's bots come in. These bots keep track of all changes made to any page and instantly revert to the "correct" version if a vandal changes information.

STRAIGHT TALK FROM TEENS: WHAT ADVICE DO YOU HAVE ABOUT CYBERBULLYING AND DIGITAL DRAMA?

Whether IRL or online, abusive and mean behaviors are not okay. Everyone plays a role in making the internet a kinder, safer place. Here's how some teens work to be good digital citizens. Feel free to add your insights too!

> I'm careful about who I follow and who follows me. I also try to make sure my posts are supportive and kind.

> I've learned that cyberbullying knows no bounds—it can happen to anyone. If you are ever the target of cyberbullying, do not go through it alone. Be sure to get help! Nobody deserves to be treated this way.

I report abusive and inappropriate accounts to social media sites. My school has an anonymous reporting line that kids use to report bullying too.

I never share or comment on mean posts. Or sometimes a simple comment like 'STOP—NOT COOL' keeps the post from spreading.

Your thoughts:

_____

_____

_____

SCREEN STORY: #CYBERKINDNESS

Like many kids and teens, Lexie sometimes feels unappreciated and excluded. Realizing that others feel this way too inspired her to do something. She started Friend Shoutout Friday, and each week, she shares her appreciation for someone on social media.

"Whenever my friends are feeling down, or I feel like they should be recognized for who they are, I find photos or videos of them that make me smile," she says. "I write what I love about them and how they've affected so many other people's lives."

Cyber kindness is the opposite of cyberbullying. It uses technology to support and help others. Through Friend Shoutout Friday, Lexie's spreading cyber kindness by the bucketload. Her friends tell her how her messages made their day. Lexie's posts also create ripples of kindness as others chime in and add more positive comments. #Cyberkindness in action!

Lexie's posts are a perfect example of how people can use their phones to make the world a kinder place. Imagine the impact if more people chose to spread kindness online. Pretty powerful stuff! How will you use your power in the digital world for good?

👽 **WEIRD FACT:**

According to the Pew Internet Research Center, "90% of social media-using teens who have witnessed online cruelty say they have ignored mean behavior on social media, and more than a third (35%) have done this frequently." This is unfortunate because, according to DoSomething.org, most bullying stops when someone intervenes.

CRACK THE SECRET CODE— CYBERBULLYING & DIGITAL DRAMA

Use the emojis below to unlock the secret code about cyberbullying and digital drama. The first word has been filled in for you to get you started.

Emoji Code

👶	human
🖤	kind
🙂	every
👀	There

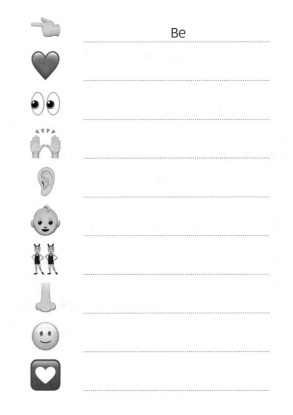	screen
	behind
	Be
	a
	being
	is

Be

SUMMARY—CYBERBULLYING & DIGITAL DRAMA

As a digital citizen, you are bound to come across cyberbullying and digital drama. Here's a checklist to help you make the internet a kinder, safer place. And remember, if you are ever feeling scared or upset by online behavior, be sure to talk to a trusted adult.

CYBERBULLYING & DIGITAL DRAMA—HEALTHY & SAFE HABITS CHECKLIST

	Screenshot or Record—Screenshot social media posts and save messages and texts when cyberbullying occurs. Turn these over to an adult who you believe can help.
	Block, Unfollow, or Leave—Block those who cyberbully from contacting you. Most apps and gaming platforms allow you to block certain users from messaging you or even being able to "see" you online.
	Report—Contact the site or platform where cyberbullying occurs and make a report. Many sites and apps make it easy to report cyberbullying. Harassment is a violation of the Terms of Service of most online spaces.

Get Help—Identify responsible adults and report the experience. Never keep to yourself the fact that you're being bullied.
Be an Upstander—Support the targets of bullying, and show cyberbullies you won't join their harassment.

WEIRD PHONE TRIVIA #8

The first webcam was created in Cambridge, England, to monitor the status of a _____ .

A. traffic intersection

B. groundhog

C. castle

D. coffee pot

Answer: D. coffee pot. The Trojan Room coffee pot was located in the Computer Laboratory of the University of Cambridge. To save people the disappointment of finding the coffee machine empty, a camera was set up, providing a live picture to all computers on the office network. When the camera was connected to the internet in 1993, the coffee pot gained international fame as the first webcam.

CHAPTER 9:

BONUS ACTIVITIES! TECHY TIDBITS, WEIRD FACTS, TRIVIA & DEFINITIONS REVISITED

STOP! If you haven't read Chapters 1-8, go back and read those chapters first. Seriously! This chapter won't make a lot of sense otherwise. Thank you for your cooperation :)

CONGRATULATIONS! You made it through eight chapters. Since your brain is bursting with knowledge about your phone, it's time to hit the pause button. Remember those techy tidbits, weird facts, definitions, and trivia questions from past chapters? Time to have some fun with them! This chapter is filled with random activities to bring those weird facts to life. Why, you ask? Well, why not?!

The First Cell Phone Meets Your Phone

A techy tidbit in Chapter 5 described the first cell phone created by Motorola. It looked like a brick with an antenna. Draw a **meme** of what the first cell phone would say upon meeting your sleek cell phone for the first time.

📌 **DEFINITION:**

Meme (noun): an amusing or interesting item (such as a captioned picture or video) that is spread widely online, especially through social media.

Bluetooth the Viking

Weird Phone Trivia #7 in Chapter 7 shared that Bluetooth technology got its name from Viking Harald "Bluetooth" Gormsson. His dead tooth earned him his nickname. Sketch what you imagine Bluetooth looked like. For bonus points, add a treasure chest filled with cell phones.

Bluetooth the Viking (Continued)

Imagine that Bluetooth and his Viking pals time-traveled to the present day and got cell phones. What would he text to his Viking pals? Fill in the text bubbles below.

ARRRGGG!

_____

_____

_____

_____

_____

NEW EMOJI TIME

In the circles, create new **emojis** for the words below. If you don't remember what a word means, revisit the definition in the chapter.

 **DEFINITION:**

Emoji (noun): small images, symbols, or icons used in electronic communication (such as text messages, email, and social media) to express the emotional attitude of the writer, convey information succinctly, or communicate a message without using words.

Draw an emoji for <u>nomophobia</u>

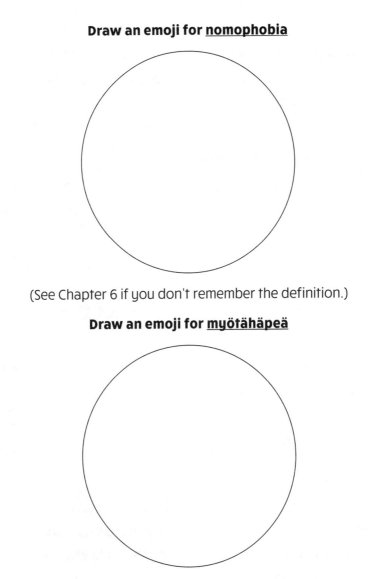

(See Chapter 6 if you don't remember the definition.)

Draw an emoji for <u>myötähäpeä</u>

(See the Introduction if you don't remember the definition.)

Create Your Own Emoji

Design a new emoji that you would like to introduce to the digital world. (BTW, a rainbow poop emoji has already been invented :)

Meaning:

_____

_____

_____

TOP 5 LISTS

There are many amazing things about having a cell phone, like connecting with friends, playing music, and more. What are your favorite things about life with a cell phone? Write your top five favorites in the list below.

Top 5 Best Things about Having a Cell Phone

1. _____

2. _____

3. _____

4. _____

5. _____

And of course, there are some not-so-great things about having a cell phone. Maybe you have a hard time putting your phone away to do homework. Or possibly you feel FOMO after scrolling through social media. What do you find hard about having a cell phone? Write your top five ideas in the list below.

Top 5 Worst Things about Having a Cell Phone

1. _____

2. _____

3. _____

4. _____

5. _____

This book explored all sorts of topics to help you navigate the digital world. The more you understand disinformation, cyberbullying, digital drama, privacy, persuasive design, and other online experiences, the better equipped you will be to develop safe and healthy phone habits. Think about the topics explored in this book. What five things were the most helpful to you? Write them in the list below.

Top 5 Things You Learned from This Book

1. _____

2. _____

3. _____

4. _____

5. _____

FAVORITE QUOTES

And last but not least, reread the quotes at the beginning of each chapter. What is your favorite superhero quote? What is your favorite Yours Truly quote? Write them below.

Best Superhero Quote in this Book:

_____

_____

_____

Best Yours Truly Quote in this Book:

_____

_____

_____

CHAPTER 10:

YOU AND YOUR PHONE–A FORCE FOR GOOD

~~~~~~

So there you have it. That little device in your pocket is pretty powerful. And how its power is used lies with you. Bum, bum, bummmmmm! (That's dramatic music, in case you were wondering.)

Luckily, you are an infinitely wise human who can use your phone as a tool for good. Your posts, comments, and what you choose to share and not share make the world a better place.

Yes, you might mess up at some point. Though you are infinitely wise, you are human. Mistakes happen. You might send a text that you later regret. Or you might post something without thinking about how it will affect your digital footprint. When mistakes happen, do your best to try to make things better. And do better next time. We are all learning as we go.

As you set off on your journey to wield your phone as a force for good, use this book as a resource. It is packed with tips and tricks to keep you safe online. If you ever experience or witness cyberbullying, stranger danger, disinformation, or just weird stuff, revisit the healthy and safe checklists at the end of each chapter. Be sure to talk to a trusted adult too.

Wait, that's A LOT of checklists! Who could possibly keep track of all those lists? Well, this is your lucky day! Below you will find all the Healthy & Safe Habits combined into one convenient checklist.

Now go forth and be a good digital citizen. May the force be with you!

YOU & YOUR PHONE: HEALTHY & SAFE HABITS CHECKLIST

	Avoid Mindless Screen Time—During screen time, ask yourself, *Am I enjoying this? Is this what I want to be doing right now?*
	Set Limits and Stay Balanced—Set daily screen limits to have time to do other activities you enjoy. Avoid keeping your phone in your bedroom while sleeping.
	Be Kind—Avoid harsh posts and criticizing others online. Have tough conversations face-to-face. Texts and DMs are easily misunderstood.

	Think Before You Post—Remember that your posts are out there for anyone to see, save, and share.
	Turn Off Notifications—Turn off notifications on apps that distract you from doing other things you could or should be doing.
	Set Privacy Settings—Check your phone settings for options such as "do not share my data." As laws and rules change, more privacy options may become available.
	Keep Your Accounts Private—Keep your social media accounts private, and use a nickname instead of your real name.
	Never Share Personal Information—Keep your name, address, phone number, birthday, social security number, passwords, parents' information, and school name private.
	Choose Strong Passwords—Make sure to use strong passwords and keep them private to avoid anyone else accessing your accounts. People get hacked all the time. Only your parents should have your passwords.

	Only Accept Friend Requests from People You Know—Some people use social media to stalk people, steal information, or cause harm.
	Remember That It's Easy for People to Pretend to Be Someone Else Online—Photos, profiles, posts, and messages can easily be faked.
	Do Not Respond to Messages from Unknown Senders—Do not open links or files in messages from strangers as they often include viruses or inappropriate content.
	Delete Old Apps and Accounts—Delete apps and accounts that you no longer use so your phone will stop updating them and collecting data.
	Be an Upstander—Support targets of bullying, and show cyberbullies you won't join their harassment. Contact the site or platform where cyberbullying occurs and make a report.

	Screenshot or Record–Screenshot posts and save messages and texts when cyberbullying occurs. Turn these over to an adult who you believe can help.
	Don't Accept That Information, Images, or Videos Are Real–Before you like or share a story or post, read more about it on a source you trust. Only share information from trusted sources. If it seems too strange to be true, it probably is.
	When Feeling FOMO, Change Your Focus, Connect with a Friend or Family, or Change Your Feed–Feelings of loneliness or exclusion are your brain's way of telling you to reach out and connect with someone. Text a friend, talk to a trusted adult, or change your feed to show you more of what inspires you.

> **Ask for Help**—We all need a little help from time to time. If you are struggling, reach out to a trusted adult, especially if
>
> - something concerning is posted about you, or you post something you wish you hadn't
>
> - you are unsure about something your read or saw online
>
> - your lonely or sad feelings persist
>
> - you are experiencing teasing or harassment online
>
> - someone sends you inappropriate photos, asks you to meet, or makes you uncomfortable.

ANSWER KEY: CRACK THE SECRET CODE

CHAPTER 1: WHY TECH COMPANIES WANT YOU STARING AT YOUR SCREEN

Code: Screen time = $ for tech, but your time is yours.

CHAPTER 2: YOUR DIGITAL FOOTPRINT (AKA YOUR DIGITAL REPUTATION)

Code: Nothing you share online is private.

CHAPTER 3: DETECTING DISINFORMATION—SLEUTHING TRUTH FROM LIES AND FAKE STUFF

Code: Just because it is shared online does not make it true.

CHAPTER 4: SOCIAL MEDIA—WELCOME TO DISNEYLAND

Code: Use social media to make the world better.

CHAPTER 5: FOMO, FOJI, AND TEXT SLANG GALORE

Code: In my humble opinion, you are great in real life. May the force be with you!

CHAPTER 6: ZOMBIE LAND—IS TECH ADDICTION A THING?

Code: Too much tech is not a good thing.

CHAPTER 7: CREEPY PEOPLE—STRANGER DANGER ONLINE

Code: When a stranger contacts you online, don't click, don't respond, and check with an adult.

CHAPTER 8: CYBERBULLYING AND DIGITAL DRAMA, UGH

Code: Be kind. There is a human being behind every screen.

A NOTE TO CAREGIVERS

To support your child as they navigate the responsibilities of having a phone, it helps to establish clear family rules and a phone contract. A cell phone contract is a written agreement between you and your child detailing how everyone will behave with their phone. It outlines your child's privileges, your family rules, and your commitment as a parent to support your child's safety and privacy. It also contains a plan for when things go wrong. Many phone contracts are available online, so you can find one that best fits your family.

You also may choose to read this book along with your child as it provides a framework for healthy and safe online habits and opens the door to important conversations about technology.

Lastly, parents play an important role in modeling healthy phone behaviors, such as putting away phones during mealtimes and family activities. Think about the tech behaviors you wish to see in your child and model these behaviors every day. Wishing you and your family the best on your tech journey!

REFERENCES

"#StatusOfMind—Social Media and Young People's Mental Health and Wellbeing." Royal Society for Public Health, May 2017. https://www.rsph.org.uk/static/uploaded/d125b27c-0b62-41c5-a2c0155a8887cd01.pdf.

"11 Facts about Bullying." DoSomething.org. https://www.dosomething.org/us/facts/11-facts-about-bullying.

"2017 Children's Mental Health Report: Smartphones and Social Media." Child Mind Institute, September 22, 2021. https://childmind.org/awareness-campaigns/childrens-mental-health-report/2017-childrens-mental-health-report/smartphones-social-media/.

Abrams, Abigail. "Your Cell Phone Is 10 Times Dirtier than a Toilet Seat. Here's What to Do about It." *Time*, August 23, 2017. https://time.com/4908654/cell-phone-bacteria/.

"Addictive Behaviours: Gaming Disorder." World Health Organization, October 22, 2020. https://www.who.int/news-room/questions-and-answers/item/addictive-behaviours-gaming-disorder.

Anderson, Monica. "A Majority of Teens Have Experienced Some Form of Cyberbullying." Pew Research Center,

September 27, 2018. https://www.pewresearch.org/internet/2018/09/27/a-majority-of-teens-have-experienced-some-form-of-cyberbullying/.

Bansal, Agam, et al. "Selfies: A Boon or Bane?" *Journal of Family Medicine and Primary Care* 7, no. 4 (2018): 828–31. https://www.ncbi.nlm.nih.gov/pmc/articles/PMC6131996/.

Berger, Jonah, and Katherine L. Milkman. "What Makes Online Content Viral?" *Journal of Marketing Research* 49, no. 2 (2012): 192–205. https://jonahberger.com/wp-content/uploads/2013/02/ViralityB.pdf.

Buckley, Chris. "China Tightens Limits for Young Online Gamers and Bans School Night Play." *New York Times*, August 30, 2021. https://www.nytimes.com/2021/08/30/business/media/china-online-games.html.

"California Privacy Rights Act: An Overview." Privacy Rights Clearinghouse, December 10, 2020. https://privacyrights.org/resources/california-privacy-rights-act-overview.

Center for Humane Technology. https://www.humanetech.com/.

Ceci, L. "Number of Monthly Active Users (MAU) of Tiktok Worldwide from January 2018 to September 2021." Statista, April 29, 2022. https://www.statista.com/statistics/1267892/tiktok-global-mau/.

"Chapter Two: Computers on Board the Apollo Spacecraft." *Computers in Spaceflight: The NASA Experience*. https://history.nasa.gov/computers/Ch2-5.html.

Chen, Jenn. "Instagram Statistics You Need to Know for 2022." Sprout Social, March 15, 2022. https://sproutsocial.com/insights/instagram-stats/.

"Computer Basics: Understanding the Cloud." GCFGlobal.org. https://edu.gcfglobal.org/en/computerbasics/understanding-the-cloud/1/.

"Cyberbullying & Digital Drama." Common Sense Education, October 1, 2017. https://www.commonsense.org/education/digital-citizenship/cyberbullying-and-digital-drama.

"CyberWise Learning Hub: Cyberbullying." Cyberwise. https://www.cyberwise.org/cyberbullying-hub.

Dizikes, Peter. "Study: On Twitter, False News Travels Faster than True Stories." *MIT News*, March 8, 2018. https://news.mit.edu/2018/study-twitter-false-news-travels-faster-true-stories-0308.

Ducharme, Jamie. "No, Teens Aren't Growing 'Skull Horns' Because of Smartphones." *Time*, April 30, 2021. https://time.com/5611036/teenagers-skull-horns/.

Dunbar, R. I. M. "Do Online Social Media Cut through the Constraints That Limit the Size of Offline Social Networks?" *Royal Society Open Science* 3, art. 150292 (2016): 1–9. https://royalsocietypublishing.org/doi/10.1098/rsos.150292.

"Fomo: How the Fear of Missing Out Drives Social Media 'Addiction.'" BBC News, March 1, 2017. https://www.bbc.com/news/technology-39129228.

Freed, Richard. "The Tech Industry's War on Kids." Medium, March 12, 2018. https://medium.com/@richardnfreed/the-tech-industrys-psychological-war-on-kids-c452870464ce.

Geddes, John. "The Process of Persuasion—How to Make a Casual Browser an Intrigued User." Interaction Design Foundation, 2020. https://www.interaction-design.org/literature/article/the-process-of-persuasion-how-to-make-a-casual-browser-an-intrigued-user.

Gonden, Rowena. "Social Media Linked to Increase in Depression among Teens, Young Adults." Healthline, March 19, 2019. https://www.healthline.com/health-news/social-media-linked-to-mental-health-disorders-in-igen-generation#What-the-study-revealed.

Graber, Diana. *Raising Humans in a Digital World: Helping Kids Build a Healthy Relationship with Technology*. New York: HarperCollins Leadership, 2019.

Graber, Diana. "Back-to-School: Why Reading and Writing Isn't Enough." Psychology Today, August 30, 2021. https://www.psychologytoday.com/us/blog/raising-humans-in-digital-world/202108/back-school-why-reading-and-writing-isn-t-enough.

Gregersen, Erik. "Martin Cooper." *Encyclopædia Britannica.* https://www.britannica.com/biography/Martin-Cooper.

Haidt, Jonathan. "The Dangerous Experiment on Teen Girls." *The Atlantic*, November 21, 2021. https://www.theatlantic.com/ideas/archive/2021/11/facebooks-dangerous-experiment-teen-girls/620767/.

Harris, Kendal. "The Dangers of Finstas." LearnSafe, February 14, 2019. https://learnsafe.com/the-dangers-of-finstas/.

Hinduja, Sameer, and Justin W. Patchin. "Standing Up to Cyberbullying: Top Ten Tips for Teens." Cyberbullying Research Center, 2018. https://cyberbullying.org/standing-up-to-cyberbullying-tips-for-teens.

Hoffman, Caitlin. "Teen Social Media Use May Increase Risk of Mental Health Problems." The Hub, John Hopkins University, September 11, 2019. https://hub.jhu.edu/2019/09/11/social-media-teen-mental-health/.

Hosokawa, Rikuya, and Toshiki Katsura. "Association between Mobile Technology Use and Child Adjustment in Early Elementary School Age." *PloS One* 13, no. 7, art. e0199959 (2018). https://www.ncbi.nlm.nih.gov/pmc/articles/PMC6059409/.

"How Do Internet Companies Profit with Free Services?" Investopedia, updated July 29, 2021. https://www.investopedia.com/ask/answers/040215/how-do-internet-companies-profit-if-they-give-away-their-services-free.asp.

"How Fake Social Media Profiles Are Fueling Scams and Getting People 'Duped out of Money.'" CBS News, October 21, 2021. https://www.cbsnews.com/news/fake-social-media-accounts/.

"Instagram Community Guidelines." Instagram Help Center. https://help.instagram.com/477434105621119/.

Joshua's Heart Foundation. https://joshuasheart.org/.

Kabir Chibber, Quartz. "How Taiwan Is Curbing Children's Daily Technology Exposure." *The Atlantic*, January 26, 2015. https://www.theatlantic.com/education/archive/2015/01/how-taiwan-is-curbing-childrens-daily-technology-exposure/384830/.

Kamenetz, Anya. "Is 'Gaming Disorder' an Illness? WHO Says Yes, Adding It to Its List of Diseases." NPR, May 28, 2019. https://www.npr.org/2019/05/28/727585904/is-gaming-disorder-an-illness-the-who-says-yes-adding-it-to-its-list-of-diseases.

Kelly, Mary Louise, and Kelly McEvers. "The First Text Message Celebrates 25 Years." NPR, December 4, 2017. https://www.npr.org/2017/12/04/568393428/the-first-text-messages-celebrates-25-years.

Kelly, Yvonne, et al. "Social Media Use and Adolescent Mental Health: Findings from the UK Millennium Cohort Study." *EClinicalMedicine* 3 (2018): 59–68. https://www.ncbi.nlm.nih.gov/pmc/articles/PMC6537508/.

Kendall, Graham. "Your Mobile Phone vs. Apollo 11's Guidance Computer." RealClearScience, July 2, 2019. https://www.realclearscience.com/articles/2019/07/02/your_mobile_phone_vs_apollo_11s_guidance_computer_111026.html.

Kesby, Rebecca. "How the World's First Webcam Made a Coffee Pot Famous." BBC News, November 20, 2012. https://www.bbc.com/news/technology-20439301.

Lieber, Chavie. "Tech Companies Use 'Persuasive Design' to Get Us Hooked. Psychologists Say It's Unethical." *Vox*, August 8, 2018. https://www.vox.com/2018/8/8/17664580/persuasive-technology-psychology.

Lippe-McGraw, Jordi. "Social Media Study Reveals You Can Only Count on 4 of Your 150 Facebook Friends." TODAY.com, February 1, 2016. https://www.today.com/health/social-media-study-reveals-you-can-only-count-4-your-t70316.

Linder, Courtney. "You're Constantly Being Stalked Online—and You Don't Even Know It." *Popular Mechanics*, January 28, 2021. https://www.popularmechanics.com/technology/security/a35353265/new-apple-app-data-tracking-tool/.

Locker, Melissa. "This Place Just Made It Illegal to Give Kids Too Much Screen Time." *Time*, Jan 26, 2015. https://time.com/3682621/this-country-just-made-it-illegal-to-give-kids-too-much-screen-time/.

Loewus, Liana. "What Is Digital Literacy?" *Education Week*, November 8, 2016. https://www.edweek.org/teaching-learning/what-is-digital-literacy/2016/11.

Madrigal, Alexis C. "Your Smart Toaster Can't Hold a Candle to the Apollo Computer." *The Atlantic*, July 16, 2019. https://www.theatlantic.com/science/archive/2019/07/underappreciated-power-apollo-computer/594121/.

McClurg, Lesley. "Is 'Internet Addiction' Real?" NPR, May 18, 2017. https://www.npr.org/sections/health-shots/2017/05/18/527799301/is-internet-addiction-real.

Miller, Caroline. "Is Internet Addiction Real?" Child Mind Institute, August 19, 2021. https://childmind.org/article/is-internet-addiction-real/.

"Mobile Phone Throwing in Finland." BBC News, August 19, 2012. https://www.bbc.com/news/av/world-europe-19310319.

Morubagal, Raghavendra Rao, et al. "Study of Bacterial Flora Associated with Mobile Phones of Healthcare Workers and Non-Healthcare Workers." *Iranian Journal of Microbiology* 9, no. 3 (2017): 143–51. https://www.ncbi.nlm.nih.gov/pmc/articles/PMC5719508/.

"New Data Shows FTC Received 2.8 Million Fraud Reports from Consumers in 2021." Federal Trade Commission, February 22, 2022. https://www.ftc.gov/news-events/news/press-releases/2022/02/new-data-shows-ftc-received-28-million-fraud-reports-consumers-2021-0.

"New Report Finds Teens Feel Addicted to Their Phones, Causing Tension at Home." Common Sense Media, May 3, 2016. https://www.commonsensemedia.org/press-releases/new-report-finds-teens-feel-addicted-to-their-phones-causing-tension-at-home.

"New Study Links Phone Use and Mental Health Issues in Teens." CBS News, July 3, 2017. https://www.cbsnews.com/video/new-study-links-phone-use-and-mental-health-issues-in-teens/#x.

Nicas, Jack. "Why Can't the Social Networks Stop Fake Accounts?" *New York Times*, December 8, 2020. https://www.nytimes.com/2020/12/08/technology/why-cant-the-social-networks-stop-fake-accounts.html.

"The Opposite of Cyberbullying–Meet Cyberkindness." #UseTech4Good, March 1, 2018. https://usetech4good.com/opposite-cyberbullying-cyberkindness/.

O'Dea, S. "U.S. Accidental Smartphone Damage Causes 2018." Statista, February 26, 2020, https://www.statista.com/statistics/959492/us-top-common-smartphone-damage-cause/.

"Origin of the Bluetooth Name." Bluetooth.com. https://www.bluetooth.com/about-us/bluetooth-origin/.

Orlowski-Yang, Jeff, director. *The Social Dilemma*. Netflix, 2020. 1 hr., 34 min. https://www.thesocialdilemma.com/.

"Our Letter to the APA." Screen Time Action Network, August 8, 2018. https://screentimenetwork.org/apa?eType=EmailBlastContent&eId=5026ccf8-74e2-4f10-bc0e-d83dc030c894.

Owens, Justin M., et al. "Crash Risk of Cell Phone Use While Driving: A Case-Crossover Analysis of Naturalistic Driving Data." AAA Foundation for Traffic Safety, January 2018. https://aaafoundation.org/wp-content/uploads/2018/01/CellPhoneCrashRisk_FINAL.pdf.

Rideout, Vicki, et al. "The Common Sense Census—Media Use by Tweens and Teens, 2021." Common Sense Media, 2022. https://www.commonsensemedia.org/sites/default/files/research/report/8-18-census-integrated-report-final-web_0.pdf.

"Partnership against Cybercrime." World Economic Forum. https://www.weforum.org/projects/partnership-against-cybercime.

Pelley, Scott. "How Fake News Becomes a Popular, Trending Topic." CBS News, March 26, 2017. https://www.cbsnews.com/news/how-fake-news-find-your-social-media-feeds/.

Perrigo, Billy. "How the EU's Sweeping New Regulations against Big Tech Could Have an Impact beyond Europe." *Time*, December 30, 2020. https://time.com/5921760/europe-digital-services-act-big-tech/.

Pope, Nick. "Here's the Baffling, Kind of Sad Reason Why All Japanese Phones Are Waterproof." *Esquire*, November 17, 2016. https://www.esquire.com/uk/culture/news/a11596/heres-the-baffling-reason-that-all-japanese-phones-are-waterproof/.

Przybylski, Andrew. "Electronic Gaming and Psychosocial Adjustment." *Pediatrics* 134, no. 3 (2024): e716–22. https://publications.aap.org/pediatrics/article-abstract/134/3/e716/74187/Electronic-Gaming-and-Psychosocial-Adjustment?redirectedFrom=PDF.

Riehm, Kira E. "Associations between Time Spent Using Social Media and Internalizing and Externalizing Problems among US Youth." *JAMA Psychiatry* 76, no 12 (2019): 1266–73. https://jamanetwork.com/journals/jamapsychiatry/fullarticle/2749480.

Rusli, Evelyn M. "Facebook Buys Instagram for $1 Billion." *New York Times*, April 9, 2012. https://dealbook.nytimes.com/2012/04/09/facebook-buys-instagram-for-1-billion/.

Sadeghi, McKenzie. "Fact Check: Bluetooth Is Actually Named after the Viking King Who United Denmark, Norway." *USA Today*, February 19, 2021. https://www.usatoday.com/story/news/factcheck/2021/02/19/fact-check-bluetooth-named-after-viking-king-harald/4505776001/.

Saul Ewing Arnstein & Lehr, LLP. "The California Privacy Rights Act of 2020: How to Comply with the Newest Privacy Law." JD Supra, November 19, 2020. https://www.jdsupra.com/legalnews/the-california-privacy-rights-act-of-24679/.

Seward, Zachary M. "The First Mobile Phone Call Was Made 40 Years Ago Today." *The Atlantic*, April 3, 2013. https://www.theatlantic.com/technology/archive/2013/04/the-first-mobile-phone-call-was-made-40-years-ago-today/274611/.

Shaer, Matthew. "What Emotion Goes Viral the Fastest?" *Smithsonian* magazine, April 2014. https://www.smithsonianmag.com/science-nature/what-emotion-goes-viral-fastest-180950182/.

Shahar, David, and Mark G. L. Sayers. "Author Correction: Prominent Exostosis Projecting from the Occipital Squama More Substantial and Prevalent in Young Adult than Older Age Groups." *Scientific Reports* 9, art. 13707 (2019). https://www.nature.com/articles/s41598-019-49153-6.

Singer, P. W., and Michael McConnell. "Want to Stop the Next Crisis? Teaching Cyber Citizenship Must Become a National Priority." *Time*, January 21, 2021. https://time.com/5932134/cyber-citizenship-national-priority/.

Smith, Kit. "50 Incredible Instagram Statistics." Brandwatch, January 20, 2019. https://www.brandwatch.com/blog/instagram-stats/.

Spada, Marcantonio M. "An Overview of Problematic Internet Use." *Addictive Behaviors* 39, no. 1 (2014): 3–6. https://pubmed.ncbi.nlm.nih.gov/24126206/.

Steinhilber, Brianna. "4 Exercises to Combat 'Text Neck.'" NBCNews.com, January 24, 2018. https://www.nbcnews.com/better/health/4-neck-exercises-will-counteract-effects-texting-ncna840291.

Sydell, Laura. "We Tracked Down a Fake-News Creator in the Suburbs. Here's What We Learned." NPR, November 23, 2016. https://www.npr.org/sections/alltechconsidered/2016/11/23/503146770/npr-finds-the-head-of-a-covert-fake-news-operation-in-the-suburbs.

"Teen Uses His Love of Baseball to Create a Positive Digital Footprint." #UseTech4Good, January 8, 2018. https://usetech4good.com/positive-digital-footprint/.

"Teens and Social Media Use: What's the Impact?" Mayo Clinic, February 26, 2022. https://www.mayoclinic.org/healthy-lifestyle/tween-and-teen-health/in-depth/teens-and-social-media-use/art-20474437.

Theoharis, Mark. "Teen Sexting." CriminalDefenseLawyer by Nolo, September 8, 2020. https://www.criminaldefenselawyer.com/crime-penalties/juvenile/sexting.htm.

Thomée, Sara. "Mobile Phone Use and Mental Health: A Review of the Research That Takes a Psychological Perspective on Exposure." *International Journal of Environmental Research and Public Health* 15, no. 12 (2018): 2692. https://www.ncbi.nlm.nih.gov/pmc/articles/PMC6314044/.

Turner, Terry. "Internet Safety for Kids." *Cyberwise*, November 17, 2021. https://www.cyberwise.org/post/internet-safety-for-kids.

Twenge, Jean M. "Have Smartphones Destroyed a Generation?" *The Atlantic*, March 19, 2018. https://www.theatlantic.com/magazine/archive/2017/09/has-the-smartphone-destroyed-a-generation/534198/.

Twenge, Jean M., et al. "Increases in Depressive Symptoms, Suicide-Related Outcomes, and Suicide Rates Among U.S. Adolescents After 2010 and Links to Increased New Media Screen Time." *Clinical Psychological Science* 6, no. 1 (2017): 2–17. https://journals.sagepub.com/doi/abs/10.1177/2167702617723376?journalCode=cpxa.

Weaver, Caity, and Danya Issawi. "'Finsta,' Explained." *New York Times*, September 30, 2021. https://www.nytimes.com/2021/09/30/style/finsta-instagram-accounts-senate.html.

Wells, Georgia, et al. "Facebook Knows Instagram Is Toxic for Teen Girls, Company Documents Show." *The Wall Street Journal*, September 14, 2021. https://www.wsj.com/articles/facebook-knows-instagram-is-toxic-for-teen-girls-company-documents-show-11631620739.

"What Is Persuasive Design?" Interaction Design Foundation. https://www.interaction-design.org/literature/topics/persuasive-design.

"What Is the Impact of Advertising on Kids?" Common Sense Media, June 4, 2020. https://www.commonsensemedia.org/articles/what-is-the-impact-of-advertising-on-kids.

Whitaker, Bill. "Synthetic Media: How Deepfakes Could Soon Change Our World." CBS News, October 10, 2021. https://www.cbsnews.com/news/deepfake-artificial-intelligence-60-minutes-2021-10-10/.

"Who We Are." Center for Humane Technology. https://www.humanetech.com/who-we-are#our-story.

Zakrzewski, Cat. "Europe to Slap New Regulations on Big Tech, Beating U.S. to the Punch." *The Washington Post*, April 22, 2022. https://www.washingtonpost.com/technology/2022/04/22/european-lawmakers-digital-services/.

Zote, Jacqueline. "130 Most Important Social Media Acronyms and Slang You Should Know." Sprout Social, August 7, 2020. https://sproutsocial.com/insights/social-media-acronyms/.

ABOUT JESSICA SPEER, AKA YOURS TRULY :)

Jessica Speer is the award-winning author of *BFF or NRF (Not Really Friends)? A Girl's Guide to Happy Friendships* and *Middle School—Safety Goggles Advised*. Blending humor, activities, stories, and practical insights, her writing unpacks the tricky stuff that peaks during the preteen and teen years.

Jessica has a master's degree in social sciences and a knack for exploring complicated topics in ways that connect with kids. She finds inspiration in superhero quotes, awkward moments, and endless cups of tea. She lives in Colorado with her husband and two daughters. For more information, visit **www.JessicaSpeer.com**.

ABOUT FAMILIUS

VISIT OUR WEBSITE: WWW.FAMILIUS.COM

   Familius is a global trade publishing company that publishes books and other content to help families be happy. We believe that the family is the fundamental unit of society and that happy families are the foundation of a happy life. We recognize that every family looks different, and we passionately believe in helping all families find greater joy. To that end, we publish books for children and adults that invite families to live the Familius Ten Habits of Happy Family Life: love together, play together, learn together, work together, talk together, heal together, read together, eat together, give together, and laugh together. Founded in 2012, Familius is located in Sanger, California.

CONNECT

   Facebook: www.facebook.com/familiustalk
   Twitter: @familiustalk, @paterfamilius1
   Pinterest: www.pinterest.com/familius
   Instagram: @familiustalk

FAMILIUS

The most important work you ever do will be within the walls of your own home.